# the
# Real Estate
# WAKE UP
## call

# the
# Real Estate
# WAKE UP
## call

Why You Must

Invest In Real

Estate Now

If You Want to

Retire Worry Free

## Carter Froelich

New York

# The Real Estate Wake Up Call

Why You Must Invest in Real Estate Now If you Want to Retire Worry Free

ISBN 978-1-60037-560-6

## MORGAN · JAMES
THE ENTREPRENEURIAL PUBLISHER

Morgan James Publishing, LLC
1225 Franklin Ave., STE 325
Garden City, NY 11530-1693
Toll Free 800-485-4943
www.MorganJamesPublishing.com

In an effort to support local communities, raise awareness and funds, Morgan James Publishing donates one percent of all book sales for the life of each book to Habitat for Humanity. Get involved today, visit **www.HelpHabitatForHumanity.org**.

# Acknowledgments

I would like to thank my wife, Bronwyn, for her support, patience, and love as I trekked the road of writing this book. Appreciation and thanks also go to my children: Curry, Logan, and Tara, for their encouragement and for reminding me what is important in life.

Lastly, I would also like to thank my parents, Don and Pat, for introducing me to real estate and for teaching me the value of integrity and hard work.

# Contents

# Chapter 1

## Do You Want a Worry-Free Retirement?

I want to begin by saying that I never planned to write a book, let alone one dealing with the issues of retirement. I am an accidental writer who stumbled upon the idea of the worry-free retirement after graduating from the University of Southern California's (USC) Masters of Real Estate Development (MRED) program. USC's MRED program was established in 1987 to prepare students for key roles in development companies.

In 1991, I was in charge of helping USC's Lusk Center to present a real estate conference in Phoenix, Arizona, and I happened to bump into a fellow MRED classmate. I asked him what development company he was working for, and he replied that he was working at a local building supply company in their plumbing department. My initial thought was that he was crazy to have just spent $30,000 on graduate school and not to have taken a job with a development company. He went on to say that he took the job because he wanted to get employee discounts on building supplies.

He had taken the money he had earned as a real estate broker in southern California and was buying single-family homes from the Resolution Trust Company (RTC) around Arizona State University

(ASU) and renting them to ASU students. He currently owned twelve homes, and his goal was to buy five more homes and have them paid off within ten years. He then planned to retire and never worry again about working, as he would live off of the rental income generated by his seventeen rental properties. At the time, I thought that this was a great idea. However, I truly began to appreciate the power of my classmate's investment strategy when I began speaking with couples who had retired and had invested their retirement savings in the stock market. They explained to me the financial challenges they were facing as a result of poor stock-market returns and insufficient monthly income without selling their stocks. Many of these retired couples' net worth had been cut in half by the tech bubble.

I began thinking that rather than following the financial industry's advice to invest in the stock market, it would make more sense to make real estate my investment foundation, which would not only increase in value over time but would also generate a recurring monthly income stream to be used in retirement.

I thought that this was a much better idea than the financial industry's approach, and when I spoke with my wife about the idea, she agreed. We began to purchase real estate as the core of our investment portfolio to allow us to have a worry-free retirement.

### *I Practice What I Preach*

I would like the reader to know that the information that I will be providing in this book is based upon my experience as a real estate investor. I am a certified public accountant in the states of Arizona and California, and I am also an Arizona state-certified general real estate appraiser. At present, I am a partner in a national real estate consulting firm.

As previously mentioned, I began my real estate investment journey in the mid-1990s in Phoenix, Arizona, when I had just started my consulting practice. I had little to no money to invest, and my credit was less than stellar. Sure, I had a job. However, we were living paycheck to paycheck, and my wife and I had very little savings with which to purchase investment properties. Not only did we have no money to invest, but both the national and Phoenix real estate markets were still reeling from the savings and loan crisis.

The RTC was taking over failing savings and loan companies and selling foreclosed properties for pennies on the dollar. I remember preparing appraisals for small apartment complexes during this time, and you could purchase apartment units in Phoenix for as low as $5,000 per unit! Today those same units are selling for over $80,000 per unit. I bring this up because the conditions in the mid-1990s, when my wife and I began investing in real estate, were similar to the conditions today. In fact, it is my opinion that a depressed real estate market is the best time to purchase real estate. If only I'd had the cash or the knowledge about how to access capital during the mid-1990s, our real estate portfolio would be much larger today.

Because I had no money to invest in real estate, I had to be creative. As they say, necessity is the mother of invention. I had my home, which was previously a homebuilder's model home that he was forced to give back to the bank. I acquired it for $98,000 with a Farmer's Home Administration (FHA) loan with 3 percent down. My first investment property was a two-bedroom, two-bathroom condominium in the White Mountains of Arizona, purchased for $48,000. I did not have the $4,800 down payment to purchase the unit, but I was able to obtain a 70-percent first mortgage from a traditional lending institution and have the seller carry back a

30-percent second mortgage. This was one of those no-money-down transactions that you see on late-night television. Carlton Sheets would have truly been proud of my investment! After three years, when the value had increased to $68,000, I was able to refinance the first mortgage and pay off the seller with an 80-percent, fifteen-year fixed mortgage at an interest rate of 4.75 percent.

The next two real estate transactions were similar in nature. I purchased a condominium unit in Phoenix and a single-family home in Phoenix with no money down. Our subsequent real estate transactions all involved making 10-percent down payments and obtaining a mortgage for the remaining purchase price. At present, my wife and I own nineteen properties, including single-family homes, condominium units, a townhome, a duplex, an office building, and beachfront residential lots. The total equity of our real estate holdings is in excess of $4 million.

The reason that I am discussing my early investment career is to make a point. *Even if your credit is in shambles and you don't have money to invest, you can still begin to amass your real estate fortune.* As I said, the depressed real estate market is the best time to purchase property. To paraphrase Warren Buffet, "Most people get interested in investing when everyone else is. The time to get interested is when no one else is. You can't buy what is popular and do well."

It is my purpose in this book to 1) explain why, in my opinion, real estate should be the cornerstone of your investment portfolio if you want to retire worry-free, and 2) provide you with the Real Estate Wealth-Building System, a proven pathway to financial security that will allow you to achieve your goals.

The key is to start today. No matter what your age, if you are willing to put in the work, you can achieve a worry-free retirement.

# Chapter 2

## Will You Be Able to Retire?

For the reasons that I will be discussing, most people who wish to enjoy the later years of their lives in retired bliss living at, or slightly below their current living standards, will never be able to so. Luckily for you, you have purchased this book in order to arm yourself with the knowledge you will need to avoid the fate that awaits a large number of Americans desiring to retire. The vast majority of people will not enjoy a comfortable retirement because they fall into one of the following four categories:

1. **Non-Savers**—These individuals spend all of their money and do not make savings a priority. As a result, they will never have money to invest in their future.

2. **Credit Lovers**—These individuals spend more money than they make, relying on credit cards and home equity loans to fuel their unsustainable living standards.

3. **Government Reliers**—These individuals do not worry about providing for their retirement, as they believe that the government will meet all of their needs.

4. **Low-Return Investors**—These individuals actually live below their means, save money, and invest for their retirement. However, they do not generate significant rates of returns on their investments to generate a substantial net worth.

If you see yourself falling into one of these categories, keep reading, as it is the purpose of this book to give you a wake-up call to what you need to do today to alter your financial course.

If you fall into category 4, this means that you are saving money and funding your retirement accounts (401(k) plans, Individual Retirement Accounts (IRAs), Roth IRAs, Superannuations, etc.), that in most cases will be invested in mutual funds, individual stocks, and bonds.

In fact, you may believe that, given the power of compound interest, you will be able to retire at your present standard of living and never have to worry about money again. This is erroneous thinking, and you may find yourself having to substantially cut your standard of living. Why? Because the vast majority of individuals within this category cannot and will not generate the necessary investment returns, create a substantial net worth, or generate a recurring monthly income with their mutual fund, stock, or bond investments to live comfortably.

Most importantly, the aforementioned investment vehicles do not generate a monthly cash flow. Sure, some of the stocks will pay dividends, and bonds will pay out principal and interest payments every six months, but this is typically not a large enough payout to allow you to live at your current standard of living. Under this retirement investment scenario, which I will be referring to as the old-school method of investing for retirement, in order to generate a monthly income to pay your living expenses, you must begin to sell off your assets (stocks, bonds, and mutual funds). This reduces your asset base and your ability to generate future monthly cash and investment appreciation. Additionally, the sales of stocks and bonds may trigger a taxable event that will force you to pay taxes, creating the necessity to sell more assets. This becomes a vicious cycle that can seriously impair your financial options.

The Vicious Cycle

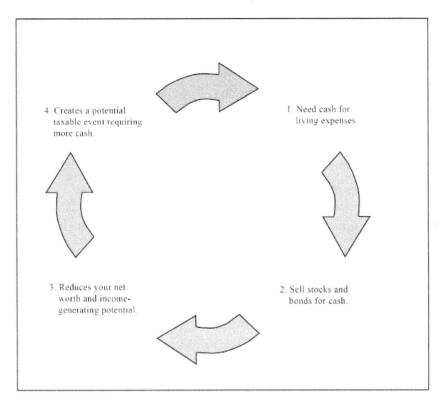

4. Creates a potential taxable event requiring more cash.

1. Need cash for living expenses.

3. Reduces your net worth and income-generating potential.

2. Sell stocks and bonds for cash.

The other factor that eats away at your ability to retire comfortably is inflation. Unless you are generating a return that is substantially higher than the core level of inflation, your purchasing power is being eroded every month. At the time this book was being prepared, the inflation rate for consumer goods and services as reported by www.inflation.com was 5.02 percent for the month of June 2008. As such, it is important that your investments generate returns that are well in excess of the rate of inflation to avoid the loss of future purchasing power.

A cautionary tale of the perils of the old-school method of investing is illustrated by the story of John and Susan. At the age of 57, John and Susan sold their business and began their retirement. As John and Susan are frugal individuals, they had saved a large sum of money through their retirement accounts. They had also received a large cash payment from the sale of their business. On the advice of their financial adviser, John and Susan had invested the majority of their money in the stock market. Initially things were going well; the stock market was soaring, the tech boom was in full swing, and companies with no earnings and nothing but a business plan were causing investors (or should I say speculators) to make millions of dollars. Everyone was happy, including John and Susan.

Then overnight, the bottom fell out of the stock market. John and Susan's net worth was cut in half. Luckily, they had not invested all of their cash in the stock market and had been smart to purchase a home in Scottsdale, Arizona. In order to survive for the next few years, they were forced to live off of their cash. When their cash became depleted, they were forced to liquidate some of their stock holdings, which further reduced their net worth. Fortunately, the Arizona real estate market was as hot as the Arizona summers, and they were able to sell their home and make a tax-free $350,000 profit due to changes in tax laws. They purchased another home and used a portion of the real estate proceeds to pay their monthly living expenses. They repeated this process four years later. Their real estate investments had saved them by providing cash to live on without having to sell more stock.

John and Susan had been schooled and advised to follow the old-school method of investing, which is to save your money in both regular equity and retirement accounts. Invest the money in the stock market, sell the appreciated stocks, and live off of the sale proceeds. This sounds like a reasonable plan, but there is a challenge with the old-school method of investing. What if the stocks don't appreciate? What happens to your retirement dreams if your net worth is cut in half overnight? What happens if you don't have any assets that can generate a monthly income on which you can live? What happens if you get sick? What happens if you run out of money? These are all pitfalls of the old-school method of investing that the financial press and financial advisers do not want to discuss with you. Well, it's time that someone talked openly and honestly about these challenges and proposed an alternative retirement investment solution.

## *The Retirement Cash-Flow Solution*

In my opinion, the only investment vehicle that will allow you to generate the investment returns, net worth, and monthly cash flow necessary to retire comfortably and worry free while also providing a hedge against inflation is real estate. For the reasons that will be discussed throughout the remaining chapters of this book, real estate should be a major pillar of your retirement investment strategy. Real estate is an investment that provides monthly cash flow and allows you to create wealth much faster than other investment vehicles. Additionally, the government provides favorable tax benefits through depreciation and operational loss write-offs. Real estate is your Retirement Cash-Flow Solution, meaning it will allow you to create a substantial net worth, while at the same time generating a monthly income stream.

In order to illustrate why real estate should be the cornerstone of your retirement investment portfolio, let's take a look at a case study of two couples in their mid-30s who are in the process of saving for retirement, the Smiths and the Greens.

## Case Study 1—*The Smiths and the Greens*

The Smiths are a very conservative couple who prefer to invest their money in things that they deem are safe and easy, such as indexed stock funds. When the Smiths retire, they hope to use the money to fund their living expenses. Accordingly, on the first day of every year, the Smiths invest $10,000 in indexed stock funds. On average, the Smiths achieve the historic annual returns of the stock market of approximately 10 percent, or $1,000 ($10,000 x 10%), for their $10,000 annual investment. Over the next thirty years, the Smiths' investment portfolio will reach a value of $1,809,434, which equates to a cash-on-cash return of 10 percent over the thirty-year period.

The Greens' retirement goal is to spend as much time as possible traveling the world upon their retirement. Because the Greens do not want to sell their assets to pay for their traveling expeditions, it is important that their retirement assets generate a monthly income so that they can pay their monthly bills and spend the rest of their money for travel.

For these reasons, the Greens are intrigued with investing in real estate. The Greens also like the fact that they can take their $10,000 investment and purchase a home for $100,000, utilizing a 90-percent loan obtained from the bank. The Greens are also not afraid of the additional work required to invest in real estate, as long as it generates a higher return.

As such, and for the purpose of this example, let's assume that the Greens take their $10,000 investment, and on the first day of the year purchase a $100,000 home with a 90-percent, fifteen-year fixed mortgage with an interest rate of 7 percent.

Let's further assume that because the Greens will have some years of negative cash flow because they are paying off their mortgages over a fifteen-year time period, they will only purchase one home per year for the next fifteen years.

The Greens are able to rent out each home for $750 per month, and their homes will appreciate at an average rate of 5 percent per year (the historic average appreciation rate for homes in the United States is approximately 6 percent per year).

For simplicity's sake, we will also assume that the Greens' tenants agree to pay all operational charges, including property taxes. As an offset to not including the payment of operating expenses, I have not taken into account the positive tax benefits of owning real estate.

Assuming the facts above, at the end of the thirty-year period, the Greens' fifteen homes will be debt free and will have an estimated net value of $4,710,330. Additionally, these homes will generate a net income for the Greens of $11,250 per month, which can be used for living and travel expenses. This equates to annual cash-on-cash return of 3,081 percent. In summary, the difference between the Smiths' and the Greens' investment portfolios at the end of thirty years is outlined below.

### Comparison of Investment Strategies

| Description | Smiths | Greens | Difference |
| --- | --- | --- | --- |
| Investment Vehicle | Stocks | Real Estate | N/A |
| Yearly Investment | $10,000 | $10,000 | $0 |
| Value of Portfolio Year 30 | $1,809,434 | $4,710,330 | $2,900,896 |
| Cash-On-Cash Return | 10% | 3,081% | 3,071% |
| Monthly Income | $0 | $11,250 | $11,250 |

If you had the ability to select the retirement strategies of either the Smiths or the Greens, whose strategy would you select? It is my belief that we would all select the Greens' strategy, as it not only produces the highest net worth at the end of thirty years, but it also generates a monthly income of $11,250, or $135,000 annually, on which to fund the Greens' living (and traveling) expenses. While some of the assumptions utilized related to the illustrate the Greens' real estate portfolio are very simplistic and do not cover all of the costs with property ownership, the fundamental concept of the example holds true—that real estate provides superior investment returns and ongoing income streams vis-à-vis other forms of investments.

Unfortunately, most individuals and families in the United States and other countries around the world are following the Smiths' strategy. As such, it is highly unlikely that the vast majority of people in the world will enjoy a comfortable retirement at their current living standard with sufficient disposable income to enjoy some of the finer things in life, such as travel and giving back to the community.

It is the purpose of this book to give you a wake-up call. Stop and look at your retirement strategy. If you do not have a significant portion of investment in real estate, you may want to consider shifting a portion of your investment funds toward real estate in order to reap the financial rewards in retirement that the Greens will be enjoying. No matter what your age or financial situation, there is still time to make real estate a meaningful component of your investment portfolio.

In the remainder of this book, I will show you why you need real estate as the cornerstone of your investment strategy and how you can use real estate to create your Retirement Cash-Flow Solution.

With your Retirement Cash-Flow Solution, you will not have to worry about common retirement problems:

1. Having no monthly income in retirement
2. Paying for living expenses
3. Selling assets to sustain your standard of living
4. Inflation eating away your assets' purchasing power
5. Having the value of your assets evaporate overnight
6. Having no estate to pass on to your heirs

### *The Real Estate Wealth-Building System*

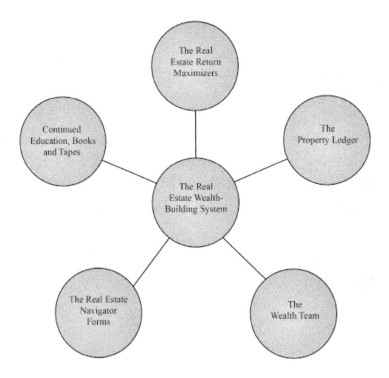

By utilizing the Real Estate Wealth-Building System, which consists of a series of unique and specialized systems and tools including the Real Estate Return Maximizers, The Property Ledger, your Wealth

Team, the Real Estate Navigator (Forms/Checklists), in conjunction with your continued education on the subject of real estate investing, you can customize your own Retirement Cash-Flow Solution. Your customized plan contains five important components:

1. A steady, reliable monthly cash flow to pay your living expenses
2. Money to fund medical and health care insurance
3. A hedge against inflation
4. A substantial net worth that can be accessed without selling the assets
5. Assets that can be passed on to your heirs

With your Retirement Cash-Flow Solution in place and providing you the solutions to the issues that plague the majority of retirees, you will have created a worry-free retirement.

What is your vision of a worry-free retirement? Utilizing the retirement vision worksheet located below, fill in the blanks to determine how many rental properties you will need to achieve your Retirement Cash-Flow Solution. Additional retirement vision worksheets, along with the Real Estate Navigator forms may be downloaded by going to www.thepropertyledger.com and clicking on the Resources tab, followed by the Reader Only Resources tab and following the directions.

## Retirement Vision Work Sheet

| Description | | Amount | Amount |
|---|---|---|---|
| Income Required During Retirement | (A) | | $ |
| Less: Estimated Social Security Payments | | $ | |
| Payouts from Pension Funds | | $ | |
| Payouts from Annuities | | $ | |
| Dividends on Stock | | $ | |
| Interest Earnings | | $ | |
| Other | | $ | |
| Other | | $ | |
| Other | | $ | |
| Other | | $ | |
| Other | | $ | |
| Subtotal | (B) | | |
| Income to Come From Real Estate | (A) - (B) = (C) | | $ |
| Average Net Income Per Residential Unit | (D) | $ | |
| Number of Rental Units Required | (C) / (D) | | $ |

# Chapter 3

## The Current Financial Landscape

Over the years we have been told by the financial press to maximize our savings into retirement vehicles including IRAs, Roth IRAs, Self-Employment Plans (SEPs), 401(k) plans, and so forth, and to invest the funds in stocks, bonds, and mutual funds. This old-school method of investing is what the Smiths were utilizing in case study 1. I agree that it is important to utilize and maximize these vehicles for tax and retirement purposes. However, for the reasons expressed in chapter 1, these investment vehicles alone will not get you to where you want to be, to a worry-free retirement.

### *Hope Is Not a Strategy!*
Some of you might be hoping that the federal government will provide for your retirement and health care needs through social security and other social programs. Unfortunately, hope is not a strategy! Given the conditions of the current economic landscape that I will discuss here, you had better *wake up a*nd begin to take action to secure your financial future.

## Current Economic Landscape
## Entitlement Mentality

I am not sure what happened to the great majority of people in the United States and other industrialized countries around the world (United Kingdom, Spain, France, Germany, Australia, etc.), but since the 1950s, we have all collectively developed a kind of complacency and entitlement mentality that the government will take care of us as we age and our physical capabilities decline. I am not saying that we are lazy, as some of the aforementioned countries have had some of the highest productivity rates ever recorded. It is just that we have come to believe too much that our politicians will be able to provide effective solutions to our current financial challenges and develop innovative vehicles to provide for the retirement and health care needs of an aging worldwide population. If this is how we as a country and global community are collectively thinking, we need to wake up! This is not going to happen, for the challenges that we face in both the United States and around the world are just too daunting. For purposes of this discussion, I will focus on the United States; however, many other countries around the world are facing one or more of the challenges enumerated below:

1. **Growing Trade Deficit**—The United States' trade deficit as of November 2007, as reported by www.trade-deficit.com, is estimated to be approximately $63.1 billion, meaning that we as a country consume more than we produce. In simple terms, it would be similar to an individual bringing home $6,000 per month to pay bills totaling $8,000 per month. If this were you or I, we all know that a day of reckoning would be coming. If we do not have enough money to pay our monthly bills or pay more than the minimum amount of the

credit card bill, interest charges will begin to compound, and our outstanding balance will grow larger and larger. At some point, chances are pretty good that we will begin missing making monthly payments on some of our obligations, and we will be remanded by the creditors for collections and possibly forced into bankruptcy.

2.  **Growing Use of Borrowed Money**—As of July 2008, the national debt of the United States totaled $9.5 trillion. Not only is the government fueling the economy with borrowed money, so are the vast majority of American families. Based upon information received from www.moneycentral.com, the average American family had more than $8,000 in credit card debt in 2004. This is more than a 167-percent increase from the average credit card debt balance in 1990. The article went on to state that the "average American household had more than $18,600 in household debt, a figure which excludes mortgage indebtedness, a 41 percent increase from that of 1998." Not only are American families spending more than they make, they are taking out debt in the form of home equity loans and multiple credit cards to fuel their preferred, albeit unsustainable, lifestyles.

3.  **Falling Dollar**—As of July 2008, the American dollar hit its lowest level in many years against other currencies. Basically, the reason the dollar is valued so low is that we as a nation consume more than we produce, and we are financing our deficit with borrowed money. As a country, in order to repay other countries and institutions from whom we borrow money, we print more money, which makes the dollar worth less than other currencies. The upshot of this is that the cost of purchasing basic goods and services will increase, and

individuals who have been saving their money in savings accounts earning an annual interest rate of 2 percent will have fewer dollars in real terms with which to purchase goods and services. Going back to our family example, as the dollar falls in value, our family falls behind and has to borrow more money to fund its lifestyle, which perpetuates the vicious cycle.

4. **Increasing Oil Prices**—As of the date of this writing in July 2008, the cost for a barrel of crude oil was $147. This represents an 86 percent increase from July 2006, when oil was $79 per barrel. Because the United States is so reliant on oil and because the United States consumes more than 25 percent of the world's oil production and has done nothing to reduce its dependence on foreign oil, we continue to drive up our trade imbalance. While the cost of oil may drop in the future, the long-term trend for oil prices will be upward given the ever-increasing demand for oil in China and India.

5. **Inflation**—Given the trade imbalance of the United States, its increasing use of debt, and recent dramatic increases in oil prices, we are seeing the reemergence of inflation as a challenge to the economy. Over the time period 2000 to 2008, the average increase in the consumer price index (CPI) was approximately 2.65 percent per annum. From the period June 2006 to June 2008, we have seen the CPI increase 4.8 percent.

6. **Low Savings Rate**—According to the United States Bureau of Economic Analysis, our savings rate (defined as savings as a percentage of disposable personal income) was .02 percent for the fourth quarter of 2007. In fact, the report went on to state that "the actual savings rate of Americans during the fourth quarter 2007 may be near zero or below zero when outlays

financed by borrowings (credit cards, equity loans) or selling investments or other assets or using savings from previous periods are taken into account." Can you believe this statistic? The average personal income for the year ending December 31, 2005, according to the United States Census Bureau, was $32,140. As such, if the average American saved 0.2 percent of this amount, his savings would amount to a whopping $64 ($32,140 × .002) per year! How can anyone expect to retire comfortably by saving $64 per year? Thankfully, prior to the third quarter of 2005, Americans experienced a higher savings rate. During the period 2000 to the third quarter of 2005, the savings rate of Americans was approximately 2 percent. Given the personal income figure of December 31, 2005, of $32,140, during this time period the average American was saving approximately $643 ($32,140 × .02) per year. During the third quarter of 2005, the savings rate dropped below zero in real terms and has remained below 1 percent through the fourth quarter of 2007.

The anemic savings rate leads to another problem: when most people are nearing the age of retirement at age 65, their median net worth (meaning assets less liabilities) according to the Board of Governors of the Federal Reserve System as of 2004 was a mere $248,700. As the average expenditure of households over 65 years of age is $32,866 (2005 United States Bureau of Labor Statistics), assuming no other sources of income this average household wealth will only provide for approximately eight ($248,700/$32,866) years of living expenses once a couple retires. With these savings rates and family net worth figures, how do people anticipate retirement? Either they are planning on working the rest of their lives, or they are assuming that the federal government will come to their rescue in the form of social security and Medicare benefits. As one will see, this may be wishful thinking.

7. **Aging Population**—Presently, the first of the baby boomers are beginning to retire. By the year 2030, it is estimated that approximately eighty million baby boomers will have retired and will be claiming their social security and Medicare benefits. Unfortunately, the money that they have paid into the social security and Medicare system is gone, and the current payroll deductions are not sufficient to cover such a huge increase in social security and Medicare benefits.

8. **Failing Federal Economic Programs**—In case you haven't heard, our social security system and Medicare programs are broken and may be on the brink of insolvency. Presently, the social security system is $25 trillion in debt, while the Medicare system is in excess of $57 trillion in debt. Collectively these are the largest debts of the United States. As of 2008, the average social security monthly benefit was $1,079 per retiree. Previously, I indicated that eighty million baby boomers are beginning to retire. Once all of the eighty million have begun to collect their monthly retirement checks of $1,079, the United States government will have to fund $86.3 billion per month just for social security benefits! How is the government going to fund a monthly bill of $86.3 billion when the system is currently not taking in enough monthly payroll taxes to fund this obligation and is already over $25 trillion in debt? Will the government borrow more money and continue to erode the value of the dollar? Clearly, this issue has to be addressed by our national

leaders. However, we have yet to see any meaningful dialogue or action by our so-called leaders in Washington.

While I am not an expert on the topics of the federal government, social security, or Medicare, I do believe that as a certified public accountant (CPA) and a financial professional, I can recognize a financial train wreck when I see one. Clearly, without some sort of drastic action on the part of our government, the social security and Medicare systems will become a huge financial wasteland. As average Americans have not been saving during their peak earning years and as they have little in the way of financial assets, it is evident that a great many Americans are depending on the federal government to solve their financial problems and to provide for them while in retirement. In fact, given the aforementioned savings statistics, it would appear that the great majority of Americans are counting on social security and Medicare to provide some, if not all, of their financial resources during retirement. But as we can see, both of these systems are deeply in debt, and it is doubtful if the retiring baby boomers will ever receive their benefits from the social security and Medicare systems as they are currently structured.

While it is not the purpose of this book to present solutions to solve the challenges faced by the United States government in relation to social security and Medicare, it is my purpose to provide a wake-up call to all Americans who wish to retire with some semblance of financial security as well as to sound the alarm signaling that chances are very good that the present-day financial security nets of social security and Medicare may no longer exist to assist them in retirement.

It is up to us every individual to take responsibility for his or her financial destiny before it is too late. As the old saying goes, "The best time to dig a well is before you need the water." It is now time that you take your shovel and start digging your financial well to provide for your financial future, as it is my opinion that you may not be able to rely on the federal government for financial assistance.

# Chapter 4

## The Old-School Method of Investing

Based upon the previous chapter, we are now aware that the social security and Medicare programs are nearing financial collapse due to their trillions of dollars in unfunded obligations. It is truly a house of cards that in the end will collapse and most likely will never be repaired to function as originally planned. On one hand, the federal government has indicated that the social security and Medicare systems are sound, but legislative actions would indicate otherwise. If the social security and Medicare systems are on strong financial ground as the government would have us believe, why has Congress continued to pass so many new laws encouraging Americans to save on their own for their retirement? It is my opinion that when the system finally does break as more and more baby boomers retire over the next fifteen to twenty-five years, Congress will be able to tell the American people that it told us to save our money in the retirement vehicles that they created, such as the SEP, IRA, 401(k), Roth IRA, and others. If we did not take advantage of these savings vehicles, then we have no one to blame but ourselves. The point is that if you believe that the federal government is going to provide you with a safe and secure retirement, you are wrong. In the end, it is up to each and every one of us to provide for our own retirement. The federal government will not be there to help us out.

Over the years, we have been told by the financial press to maximize our savings into retirement vehicles including IRAs, Roth IRAs, Self-Employment Plans (SEP), 401(k) plans, and others and invest the funds in stocks, bonds, and mutual funds. This old-school method of investment is what the Smiths were utilizing. While I agree that it is important to utilize and maximize these vehicles for tax and retirement purposes, for the reasons expressed in chapter 1, these investment vehicles alone will not get you to a worry-free retirement. The old-school method of investing does not create the powerful financial engine that is required to generate significant net worth and the ongoing, recurring monthly cash flow required for a worry-free retirement. For you to better understand some of the limitations of the old- school method of investing, let's pull back the curtain on the old-school method of investing as Toto did in the *Wizard of Oz* to expose that the great and powerful Oz was nothing more than a traveling salesman.

### *The Limitations of the Old-School Method of Investing*

The following represent the major challenges that I see with the old-school method of investing and its ability to provide for a worry-free retirement.

**1. Lack of Leverage**—For the most part, the old-school method of investing does not allow for the use of leverage. When you purchase $10,000 worth of stock, on the day the stocks are purchased, you must pay $10,000 in cash to purchase the stocks. Thus, if the stocks return 10 percent in the first year, you receive $1,000 ($10,000 x 10%). While a 10 percent return on investment is not bad, as you saw in Case Study 1, it will not generate the types of returns that are necessary to create a significant net worth, nor will it provide you with a source of recurring monthly income.

**2. No Control over Assets**—Once you purchase a stock, bond, or mutual fund, there is nothing you can do to help the stock, bond, or mutual fund increase in value. In fact, the holders of such instruments are completely at the mercy of the management of the companies, the stock market, and the economy. There is no better example of this lack of control issue than Enron. At one point, Enron was the hottest company in the United States, named by *Fortune Magazine* for six consecutive years as one of America's most innovative companies. In August 2000, its stock hit a value of $90. Within one year, the company was in bankruptcy due to the revelation that Enron's management had participated in systematic and institutionalized accounting fraud.

**3. Limited Monthly Cash Flow**—For the most part, equities produce little to no recurring monthly income. Some stocks will pay dividends on a yearly basis, and bonds will pay a return of principal and interest every six months. However, unless you have a substantial investment in the stock and/or bond, these amounts will generally be insufficient to provide a meaningful amount of income on which to live while in retirement. As discussed earlier in the book, most Americans will never have sufficient capital to invest in income-producing securities that will provide for living expenses during retirement.

**4. No Tax Advantages**—With the exception of the investment in tax-exempt municipal bonds, investing in equities and debt instrument provides no tax advantages to the average investor. These types of investment vehicles offer the investor no ability to offset ordinary and/or passive income. Obviously, the exception to this statement is the investment of funds into your IRA, 401(k), SEP, etc.

**5. Taxable Events**—Other than obtaining dividend payments and/or semiannual payments of principal and interest related to bonds, the only way to generate cash flow from equities and debt instruments is to sell the security, which may cause a taxable event requiring you to pay ordinary income and/or capital gains tax. Accordingly, there may be no way to generate additional cash without triggering a taxable event. (Note: The one exception to this statement is if you were to take a margin loan against the investment value of your portfolio value. However, this can be an extremely risky proposition.)

**6. Buying Below Market Value**—The securities market dictates every day at what price it is willing to sell a particular stock or bond instrument. As such, when you purchase $50,000 in stock for instance, it will be worth $50,000. From that point forward, the stock and/or bond will begin to move up and down pursuant to the dictates of the market. As such, there is no way to purchase stocks and/or bonds at prices that are below what the market dictates at any particular point in time.

**7. Purchasing Power Erosion**—Stocks and bonds tend to go up or down with the dictates of the market. To the extent that the economy is experiencing bouts with inflation there exists the possibility that the purchasing power of the funds invested in stocks and bonds will be eroded, and the investor's ability to purchase goods and services with the funds invested in the stocks and bonds will be diminished. At the time this writing was going to print in December of 2008, the Dow Jones industrials have dropped to approximately 8,400, which is comparable with the Dow Jones average in January of 1998, and it is appearing that the stock market may continue its sporadic movements in the future, given the challenges to the economy created by the sub-prime lending crisis. While oil and gas prices have fallen from the summer of 2008 highs of $147 per barrel of oil and $4.37 per gallon of gas; the long-term outlook for both the prices of oil and gas remains upward, which will cause the price of consumer goods to increase over time. Given the one-two punch of decreased stock market values combined with increasing inflation, the purchasing power of the assets invested in the stock market has been seriously impaired. As one can see, the old-school method of investing does not provide an automatic hedge against inflation.

**8. Estate Planning**—There is a limited amount of estate-planning techniques that can be utilized to pass on the value of stocks and bonds to your heirs. To the extent that such assets are not included in trusts or exceed the amount of the current estate tax exemptions, your heirs may have to pay tax on the amount of the assets received, potentially creating financial challenges for them.

Keeping in mind the aforementioned limitations, the old-school method of investing does provide a means of accumulating and growing capital for retirement and is a far cry from those individuals who are doing nothing and hoping that the federal government will care for them in retirement. The old-school method of investing for retirement takes discipline, and for this strategy to be effective, you must invest the maximum amount of funds into retirement vehicles as early in the calendar year as possible and begin saving at the earliest point in your life in order to get the full benefit of the compounding interest and investment returns. Additionally, the returns to be generated by investing in stocks, bonds, and mutual funds are unpredictable given the dictates of the stock market and the lack of control that investors have over this type of investment. As we saw in chapter 1 with the Smiths, investing $10,000 per year at the beginning of the year and generating a 10-percent annualized rate of return will produce $1,809,439 over a thirty-year period.

While this is a substantial sum of money, it may not be sufficient to produce a worry-free retirement.

In my opinion, the most efficient way to create wealth and income predictability is through real estate in general and the Real Estate Wealth-Building System in particular.

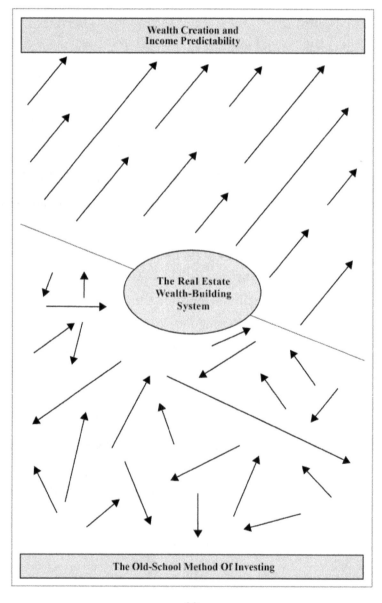

# Chapter 5

## Real Estate—
## A More Powerful Investment Vehicle

As one will recall from chapter 1, the Smiths' plan for investing for retirement has been to invest $10,000 annually into various retirement and other equity accounts in January of every year so as to put their money to work as early in the year as possible to take maximum advantage of the effects of compound interest and magnify the returns of their portfolio. If the Smiths are able to generate the annual average return for equity instruments of approximately 10 percent over a thirty-year period, their investment portfolio will be worth approximately $1.8 million. In relative terms, this is a fairly substantial amount of money. Financial advisers everywhere would applaud and compliment the Smiths for following their standard investment advice of investing funds in the debt and equity markets through standard investment vehicles, most of which have to be purchased from them.

However, if you compare the Smiths' investment results to those of the Greens', who invested their money in real estate, there is no comparison. Not only did the Smiths' net worth exceed the Greens' by $2.9 million, they received a 3,071 percent higher cash-on-cash return than the Smiths and were earning a monthly income of approximately $11,500 upon retirement, as opposed to the Smiths' monthly income of $0.

If it is your desire to have a substantial net worth with ongoing monthly income flowing into your pockets without having to sell assets, then you must seriously consider real estate as a cornerstone of your investment strategy.

## *Why Invest In Real Estate?*

Why should you include real estate in your investment portfolio? My response to this question is that real estate is the only investment vehicle that individuals of any financial means may use to create a huge net worth and also generate a significant monthly income that can fund their lifestyle.

## *Purpose of This Book*

With this having been said, I want to caution you that what I am going to be discussing during the rest of this book is not a get-rich-quick scheme. You will have to work if you want financial freedom and a worry-free retirement.

This book is for individuals who want to take control of their financial destinies and are no longer willing to sit back and assume that the federal government and/or an inheritance will fund their retirement or help them reach any other financial goals they may have established.

This book is not set up as how-to book. There have been many of these types of books written over the years that you may find at your local bookstore. Over the course of my real estate investing career, I have read and/or listened to hundreds of real estate and business books to continue to further my financial education. It has always been my goal to pick up at least one piece of meaningful information and/or technique that I could utilize immediately in my day-to-day real estate investment career. To that end, I have always been able to find at least one hint, pointer, idea, and/or strategy with which to fuel my real estate educational growth. I highly recommend that if you are truly serious about real estate investing that you read or listen to at least one book per month with the goal of gleaning at least one practical application that you can implement immediately in your real estate investing.

The key is to start today! You must make the crucial decision of whether to choose financial freedom through real estate or to accept potential financial dependency. No one will go out and do this for you. You have to take the action to begin to take control of your financial future and begin the foundation of your worry-free retirement. The journey of one thousand miles begins with the first step, so take the first step. Begin reading books on real estate investing, print out the Real Estate Navigator forms found at www.thepropertyledger.com (Resources) and begin to explore your neighborhood and surrounding area to become familiar with the real estate market. Talk to local real estate professionals working in your area. Join a local real estate investment club (go to www.reiclubs.com for a real estate club near you). Do something to begin your Retirement Cash-Flow Solution.

**FREEDOM**

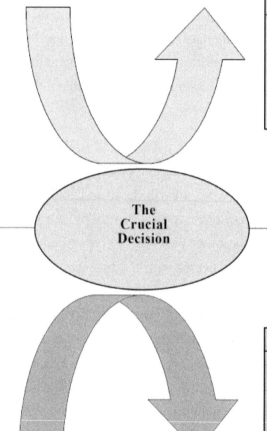

### Wealth and Income Creation

The Real Estate Wealth Building System allows you to generate huge returns with a monthly cash flow in order to achieve your Retirement Cash Flow Solution.

## The Crucial Decision

### Commoditization

Choosing the Old School Method of Investing puts you at the mercy of an unpredictable market and prevents you from generating the superior returns and cash flow which will propel you to a secure and *Worry Free Retirement.*

**DEPENDENCY**

Be advised that the journey you are about to embark on is a long journey that will be full of challenges. However, the rewards of the Real Estate Wealth-Building System of 1) taking control of your financial destiny, 2) developing a non-entitlement mentality, 3) increasing your financial, real estate, and business knowledge, 4) increasing your net worth, 5) creating a stable monthly income, and 6) developing your financial security, far outweigh the potential obstacles you may experience along the way. With that in mind, let's begin your journey to financial self-reliance by discussing the building blocks that will be both the cornerstone and the keystone to your worry-free retirement—real estate.

# Chapter 6

## The Advantages of
## Real Estate Investing

As I will discuss in this chapter, for you to develop your worry-free retirement, acquiring real estate has to be at the core of your financial strategy. Otherwise you will not generate the types of financial results required to generate a significant net worth on an ongoing cash-flow stream.

The press and financial institutions have continually preached to us that the only way to retire rich is to invest in stock and bonds, preferably with their specific institution's brokers, mutual funds, and/or retirement accounts. While I do believe that these types of financial instruments have a place in your financial strategy, they do not have the financial horsepower that you will require if you are to have a worry-free retirement. The Real Estate Return Maximizers are advantages of real estate investing that the old-school investment advisers would rather you not know about. Why? Because armed with the following facts and knowledge, you will be less inclined to rely upon the old-school method of investing to achieve your financial goals.

The Real Estate Return Maximizers

The ten Real Estate Return Maximizers that provide the fuel for the Real Estate Wealth-Building System and ultimately fund your Retirement Cash-Flow Solution are outlined here:

**1. Real Estate Allows the Use of Leverage**—Real estate is the only investment vehicle that I am aware of where banks and/or private investors are happy to lend money for your investment purposes. Financial institutions and/or private investors are happy to lend anywhere from 80 percent to 100 percent of the purchase price of real estate to investors, provided the investor has reasonably good credit. The ability to use other people's money (OPM) is called leverage. Typically, the more of the purchase price you finance with OPM, the higher the interest rate. For instance, there are private lenders in the Phoenix market who are willing to lend one hundred percent of the purchase price of investment properties. However, the terms are fifteen percent interest and a maximum term of six months. I personally do not recommend pursuing these types of loans, as they can lead to potential disaster if you cannot refinance the initial purchase mortgage. The fact that you are able to use OPM to fund your real estate investments allows you to supercharge your investment returns, as we will explore later. This is not the case with other investment vehicles. Can you imagine going into your bank and asking the banker to lend you 90 percent of the market value of Google and Microsoft stocks that you would like to purchase? The banker would not only laugh you out of the office, but he might also ask that you check yourself into a hospital for overnight observation!

Let's explore the concept of leverage as it relates to investing $50,000 in either stocks or real estate. If you purchase stocks, you will invest your money, and upon purchasing your stocks, you will have $50,000 in stocks at the end of the day (assuming they do not change in price by the close of the day). The second investment alternative is to invest the $50,000 into real estate. Because the banks are willing to lend you 90 percent of the purchase of your real estate investments, you could acquire $500,000 ($50,000/10 percent) worth of rental properties with your $50,000 investment. Thus, the use of leverage allows you to control $450,000 ($500,000 real estate - $50,000 stocks) more assets that will appreciate over time as well as generate a monthly income, provided you had purchased wisely and rented the unit for more than your monthly expenses. Why are lending institutions willing to loan up to 90 percent of the purchase price to acquire property? The answer is that real estate is considered a safe and secure investment. A further indication of the security of real estate in the eyes of lending institutions is the interest rate that they are willing to loan money to purchasers of real estate. As you know, bankers charge interest rates that are set in relation to the security securing the loan and the perceived risk they see in being repaid. At present, the interest rate being charged on real estate (6.5 percent) is much less than that of business loans (10 percent), which is much less than interest rates being charged on credit cards (18 percent). Leverage is one of the most important factors in generating and turbo charging our financial return related to our worry-free retirement. Let's now explore the use of leverage as it relates to how real estate provides superior investment returns over other investments such as stocks.

**2. Real Estate Provides Superior Investment Returns—** Continuing with our example above of investing $50,000 in stocks or purchasing $500,000 in investment property and ignoring the other positive attributes of real estate, including tax benefits and monthly rental income, real estate provides superior rates of return to stocks and other assets given the underlying power of leverage. Let's assume that over a ten-year period, the stocks appreciate in value at the historical average annual rate of return for stocks of 10 percent. At the end of the ten-year period, the value of your stock portfolio will be $129,687, which represents a total return of 159 percent over the period. Not bad, right?

Now let's investigate the real estate side of the equation. Assume that your real estate investment of $500,000 increases in value at the historical average of 6 percent per year over the same ten-year period. At the end of the ten-year period, your real estate investment portfolio will be worth $895,424, equating to a return of 791 percent over the ten-year period! The table below illustrates the difference between the stock and real estate investment vehicles over the ten-year analysis period.

| Leverage - The Real Estate Return Supercharger | | | | | | | |
|---|---|---|---|---|---|---|---|
| Year | Stock | (A) Appreciation | Annual Return On $50,000 Investment | Real Estate | (B) Appreciation | Annual Return On $50,000 Investment | (B) - (A) Difference Between Stocks and Real Estate |
| 0 | $50,000 | NAP | NAP | $500,000 | NAP | NAP | NAP |
| 1 | $55,000 | $5,000 | 10% | $530,000 | $30,000 | 60% | $25,000 |
| 2 | $60,500 | $10,500 | 21% | $561,800 | $61,800 | 124% | $51,300 |
| 3 | $66,550 | $16,550 | 33% | $595,508 | $95,508 | 191% | $78,958 |
| 4 | $73,205 | $23,205 | 46% | $631,238 | $131,238 | 262% | $108,033 |
| 5 | $80,526 | $30,526 | 61% | $669,113 | $169,113 | 338% | $138,587 |
| 6 | $88,578 | $38,578 | 77% | $709,260 | $209,260 | 419% | $170,682 |
| 7 | $97,436 | $47,436 | 95% | $751,815 | $251,815 | 504% | $204,379 |
| 8 | $107,179 | $57,179 | 114% | $796,924 | $296,924 | 594% | $239,745 |
| 9 | $117,897 | $67,897 | 136% | $844,739 | $344,739 | 689% | $276,842 |
| 10 | $129,687 | $79,687 | 159% | $895,424 | $395,424 | 791% | $315,737 |

**Assumptions**

| | |
|---|---|
| Stock Investment | $50,000 |
| Annual Appreciation on Stocks | 10% |
| Real Estate Investment | $50,000 |
| Annual Appreciation on Real Estate | 6% |

Assuming that you invested your $50,000 in real estate rather than stocks, at the end of the ten-year period you would be $315,737 wealthier in just appreciation differences than you would have been had you invested your money in stocks. Are you beginning to see why you need to consider real estate as the cornerstone of your investment portfolio?

The following is a real-life example of the power of leverage and its effect on investment returns. Jeff and Susan, who reside in Colorado, wanted to purchase two rental properties in Arizona as part of their retirement plan. They purchased a three-bedroom, two-bath single-family home in North Phoenix in 2000 for $148,000 with a $15,000 down payment and a $133,000 loan. They also purchased a three- bedroom, two-bath single-family home in Gilbert, Arizona, for $175,000 with an $18,000 down payment and a $157,000 loan. Today, even though the Phoenix housing market has experienced a decline over the last two years, the North Phoenix home is now valued at $275,000, while the Gilbert home is appraised at $300,000. As a result of utilizing OPM and purchasing two rental properties, Jeff and Susan have experienced a $252,000 [($275,000 + $300,000) - ($133,000 + $157,000)] increase in their net worth, which equates to a 764 percent ($252,000 / $33,000) return on their cash investment in the rental properties!

**3. Real Estate Produces Monthly Income**—Real estate utilized for investment purposes (with the exception of land unless leased) produces rental income to offset the costs of ownership, maintenance, and financing costs. Obviously, it is the goal of all real estate investors to have a positive cash flow after paying all operating expenses, including financing costs for all properties. While some stocks offer dividends, and bonds provide principal and interest payments, they do not provide these funds at a high enough yield to propel you to your worry-free retirement. When discussing the concept of income as it relates to investment, it is necessary to discuss the concept of yields.

Yield is defined as the ratio of annual income generated by assets, divided by the dollar amount of the investment. Often the national press will report the yields of various investment alternatives, and in my mind they present misleading information related to the yields generated by real estate versus other investment vehicles, primarily that of stocks. For instance, the news media may indicate that the yield of real estate investment for the year was 8 percent versus 15 percent for stocks. The challenge with these types of press reports is that they do not represent a comparison of apples to apples but rather apples to oranges. To truly understand the concept of income and yield, you must get into the details. So let me put on my CPA hat for a minute, and let's pull back the curtain on the press' portrayal of yield.

### Stock Yield

Assuming that you invest $10,000 in the purchase of stock, you will expend a total of $10,000 and receive stock certificates on the day of purchase for $10,000. If the stock pays a dividend of $1,500, your yield on that particular investment will be 15 percent ($1,500/$10,000).

### Real Estate Yield

In order to estimate the yield on a real estate investment, the calculation is not as simple as that of the stock, given the fact that we have utilized OPM and are incurring expenses to operate the rental property. Assuming that you have the same $10,000 to invest, you will be able to purchase a $100,000 investment property (assuming a 90-percent loan). Assuming that the real estate assets yields 8 percent, the real estate asset will produce $8,000 in rental income, or 8 percent times the home price of $100,000. However, given the fact that you have only invested $10,000 to purchase the real estate, your gross yield is much more than the 8 percent. It is actually 80 percent ($8,000 / $10,000).

In order to be truly comparable, if you are going to consider leverage in your yield analysis, you also need to take into account the fact that you have to pay the debt service on your $90,000 mortgage in addition to operating expenses. Additionally, you have to factor in the tax advantages that will accrue to you as the result of investing in real estate. One of the tax benefits that the government gives real estate investors is depreciation. Depreciation is an accounting principal that spreads the cost of an asset over its useful life. It is an attempt to match the cost of the asset with the income it produces over the predetermined useful life period established by the government. As of the date of this writing, the depreciable life of residential property is 27.5 years, while commercial property is 39 years. Depreciation is calculated based upon the depreciable cost of your investment, which is the cost of the asset less the value of the land (land is not considered an asset that loses its value) over the depreciable life of the property (i.e., 27.5 or 39 years). The beauty of depreciation is that while the government allows depreciation to reduce the income generated by your rental property, for tax purposes, however, it does not require a cash outflow.

Additionally, we have to make an adjustment for the payment of debt service related to your mortgage. For tax purposes, you are only able to deduct interest payments from your taxable income. As such, we have to back out the payment of principal related to your mortgage.

The table below on yield analysis illustrates the calculation of yields between stock and real estate. In the case of real estate I have illustrated: 1) the gross yield, 2) the yield of the property after taking into account operating expenses, depreciation, mortgage interest payment, as well as the corresponding tax benefits, and 3) the yield of the property after taking into account operating expenses once the mortgage has been paid off along with the corresponding tax benefits.

| Yield Analysis | | | |
| --- | --- | --- | --- |
| **Description** | | **Stocks** | **Real Estate** |
| Initial Investment | (A) | $10,000 | $10,000 |
| Home Purchase Price (1) | (B) | | $100,000 |
| Yield on Investment | (C) | 15% | 8% |
| Cash Returned - Stock | (A) x (B) = (D) | $1,500 | |
| Cash Returned - Real Estate | (B) x (C) = (E) | | $8,000 |
| **Gross Yield** | | | |
| Stocks | (D) / (A) | **15%** | |
| Real Estate | (E) / (A) | | **80%** |
| **Yield Calculation Including Operating Expenses** | | | |
| Gross Income | (E) | | $8,000 |
| Less: Operating Expenses (2) | (F) | | ($900) |
| Less: Mortgage (3) | (G) | | ($6,892) |
| Net Operating Income | (E) - (F) - (G) = (H) | | $208 |
| Plus: Tax Advantages (4) | (I) | | $548 |
| Total Cash Benefit | (H) + (I) = (J) | | $756 |
| **Net Real Estate Yield** | (J) / (A) | | **7.6%** |
| **Yield Calculation After Mortgage Payoff** | | | |
| Gross Income | (E) | | $8,000 |
| Less: Operating Expenses (2) | (F) | | ($900) |
| Less: Mortgage (3) | | | $0 |
| Net Operating Income | (E) - (F) = (K) | | $7,100 |
| Less: Taxes Payable (5) | (L) | | ($2,343) |
| Total Cash Benefit | (K) + (L) = (M) | | $4,757 |
| **Revised Real Estate Yield** | (M) / (A) | | **48%** |

Footnotes
(1) Assumes that a 90% loan was obtained
(2) Assumes $900 for property taxes
(3) Assumes a $90,000 mortgage, 6.5% interest rate, 30 year term
(4) Depreciable Basis

| | | |
| --- | --- | --- |
| Purchase Price | | $100,000 |
| Less: Land Value (20%) | | ($20,000) |
| Depreciable Base | (W) | $80,000 |
| Depreciation Per Year | (W) / 27.5 = (Y) | $2,909 |

Calculation of Taxable Income

| | | |
| --- | --- | --- |
| Operating Income Before Debt Service | | $7,100 |
| Less: Interest Paid for Year | | ($5,850) |
| Less: Depreciation | (Y) | ($2,909) |
| Taxable Income | | ($1,659) |
| Tax Rate | | 33% |
| Tax Benefit | | ($548) |

(5) Net Income

| | | |
| --- | --- | --- |
| Net Income | | $7,100 |
| Less Depreciation (Fully Depreciated) | | $0 |
| Taxable Income | | $7,100 |
| Tax Rate | | 33% |
| Taxes Payable | | $2,343 |

As you can see from the analysis, the determination of yield as it relates to real estate can be fairly complicated. The point of this exercise is to make you aware that what is reported in the press may not necessarily be a fair representation of the facts. Given the fact that you can use leverage to purchase real estate assets allows you to generate a huge gross yield on your investment. In our example, the gross yield of real estate compared to that of stocks was 80 percent for real estate versus 15 percent for stocks. This is much more than what the press was reporting in our example for real estate of 8 percent. After including the costs of property ownership (in our case I assumed that the property owner was only responsible for property taxes and insurance as well mortgage payments), and the tax benefits the property owner enjoys associated with real estate, we see that your net yield was approximately 7.6 percent. Once the mortgage on the property is paid off, the net yield increases to 48 percent. It is also important to remember that in the calculations above I have only looked at the income side of the various assets, and I have not considered the effects of yearly appreciation, which as they relate to real estate, can be huge. I have also assumed that rental income will remain constant over the life of the rental property, which is typically not the case. Depending upon your particular market, rental rates can generally be expected to increase between 2 to 5 percent per year. This is typically not the case in relation to dividends on stocks, which are paid out based upon a certain dollar amount per share of stock and are typically linked to the financial performance of the company.

It is important to understand that the yield calculation as the income that will be generated once the mortgage has been paid off is the second key ingredient to your worry-free retirement. What other assets can you think of that produce an annual yield of approximately 48 percent? Real estate is the only vehicle I am aware of that will produce this type of yield on a consistent basis. Are you beginning to see why it is important to have real estate holdings as the core component of your retirement holdings? Only by generating yields of 50 percent will you be able to retire worry free and not be reliant on the government or have to lower your standard of living. The goal of worry-free retirement is to grow a huge net worth through real estate and have those investments generate a net monthly positive cash flow for our retirement years. One of the most compelling factors of owning rental properties is that every morning your tenants get up to go to work so that they can pay down your mortgage, and once the mortgage has been paid off, that money (after paying operating costs) will go into your pocket to fund your retirement, pay down other investment properties' mortgages, fund your retirement lifestyle, and/or create additional wealth or allow you to give back to the community.

**4. Appreciation**—Since records have been kept in relation to the appreciation of single-family homes, they have increased in value at an average rate of approximately 6 percent per year, or approximately twice the rate of inflation. As such, not only does real estate appreciate over time, it also provides an excellent hedge against inflation. The graph below, utilizing the housing price index provided by the United State Census Bureau, provides an illustration of how a house costing $100,000 in 1975 appreciated to a value of over $501,000 in 2008, given the positive effects of appreciation.

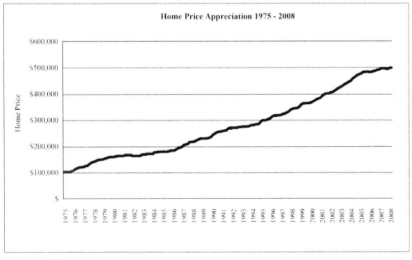

Source: U.S. Census Bureau

It should also be noted that real estate has never decreased in value nationwide. Sure, specific markets have experienced declines over the years. However, the nation as a whole has never experienced a complete loss of value. As of the date of this writing in July 2008, the national press is busy reporting on the terrible state of the real estate market and how homeowners are losing their homes to foreclosure, yet many states are reporting increases in home values as the table below illustrates.

| State Appreciation Rates 1Q 2007 - 1Q 2008 | |
| --- | --- |
| **State** | **Appreciation Rate** |
| Wyoming | 6.30% |
| Utah | 5.60% |
| Montana | 4.90% |
| Texas | 4.70% |
| Alabama | 4.50% |
| California | -10.60% |
| Nevada | -10.30% |
| Florida | -8.10% |
| Arizona | -5.10% |

Source: Office of Housing Enterprise Oversight

Combining leverage with appreciation produces huge returns, as was previously illustrated in the table included under Section 2, "Real Estate Provides Superior Investment Returns." Review Section 2 again to see how appreciation, coupled with the powerful return supercharger of leverage, produces a 791-percent return for real estate versus the 159-percent return for stocks.

**5. Amortization**—On a monthly basis, tenants make their rental payments, and you utilize their rental payments to pay down the mortgage on the property, thereby increasing your equity in the property and increasing your net worth. The table below takes the information included in Section 2, "Real Estate Provides Superior Investment Returns," and adds the yearly equity generated by the principal reductions of the outstanding mortgage. As you can see, your previous return of 791 percent has now been increased to 931 percent when you factor in the effect of paying down the outstanding mortgage balance.

What is great about the increase in returns is that other people are working for you to pay down the mortgages on your investment properties and propel you to a worry-free retirement.

| | | (A) | (B) Total Mortgage Principal Reduction | (A) + (B) | Return On $50,000 Down Payment |
|---|---|---|---|---|---|
| Year | Value of Property | Total Appreciation | | Total Equity | |
| 0 | $500,000 | $0 | $0 | $0 | NAP |
| 1 | $530,000 | $30,000 | $5,210 | $35,210 | 70% |
| 2 | $561,800 | $61,800 | $10,758 | $72,558 | 145% |
| 3 | $595,508 | $95,508 | $16,667 | $112,175 | 224% |
| 4 | $631,238 | $131,238 | $22,961 | $154,199 | 308% |
| 5 | $669,113 | $169,113 | $29,663 | $198,776 | 398% |
| 6 | $709,260 | $209,260 | $36,801 | $246,061 | 492% |
| 7 | $751,815 | $251,815 | $44,403 | $296,218 | 592% |
| 8 | $796,924 | $296,924 | $52,499 | $349,423 | 699% |
| 9 | $844,739 | $344,739 | $61,121 | $405,861 | 812% |
| 10 | $895,424 | $395,424 | $70,304 | $465,728 | 931% |

The Effect of Leverage and Amortization on Real Estate Returns

**Assumptions**

| | |
|---|---|
| Property Price | $500,000 |
| Down Payment Percentage | 10% |
| Total Down Payment | $50,000 |
| Loan Amount | $450,000 |
| Annual Appreciation Rate | 6% |
| Interest Rate | 6.50% |
| Term of Mortgage (Years) | 30 |
| Annual Payment | $34,460 |

## 6. Ability to Purchase Real Estate Below Current Market Value

—Another major benefit of investing in real estate over other assets, especially stocks, is that you can purchase real estate below its fair market value. This is not the case with stocks, as the market dictates on a daily basis the price at which holders of the stock are willing to sell their shares of XYZ Company. For instance, if the stock market price for XYZ Company is $150 per share, there is no possible way that you can purchase a share of XYZ Company for $100. As such, if you want to buy XYZ Company on this particular day, you will have to pay $150 per share. If you thought that the value for the company was only $100, and as such were only willing to pay $100 per share, you would have to check the stock market every day until the price of XYZ Company dropped to $100 per share. This could take one day or 10 years. There is no telling when the stock may drop to $100, as the stock market will dictate when this will occur. Additionally, you cannot call the management of XYZ Company on the phone and offer them $100 per share for their stock. You have to go through the stock market. As such, it is impossible to acquire on any given day stock a value below what the market is willing to take for the stock.

With real estate, however, on any given day there may be properties for sale that are well below their fair market value given the sales of similar properties. How can this happen? Why would someone sell a piece of real estate far below its fair market value? The answer is simple—it's called life. Individuals and families alike go through personal and financial changes that, from time to time, can result in the sale of assets far below their fair market value. One of the biggest life events that causes individuals to sell their property below fair market value is divorce. Often when couples are going through a divorce, they want to sell their mutual property as quickly as possible so that they can go their separate ways.

In such situations, is it possible to purchase a house worth $300,000 for $200,000? Absolutely it is. In such a situation, using the power of leverage for just $20,000 down, or 10 percent coupled with a 90-percent mortgage, one will instantly create $120,000 equity in the home ($300,000 value - $180,000 mortgage), which equates to a cash-on-cash return of 500 percent ($100,000/$20,000)! Real estate is the only investment vehicle that I know of that will allow investors instant equity and huge cash-on-cash returns. This is the type of advantage that allows you to achieve your worry-free retirement.

**7. Ability to Increase the Value of Your Real Estate Assets**—One of the huge differences between stocks and real estate is that with real estate you have the ability to increase the value of the property by your personal efforts. This is not the case with stocks. If you purchase $50,000 in stocks, there is nothing you can do personally to increase the value of the stock. You are at the mercy of the company's board of directors, management, and the consumers who purchase the product of the company. In fact, as owners of Enron stock found out, the value of stock can evaporate overnight. Think of what the owners of General Motors stock must currently be thinking given the company's decision to base the core of its business on large trucks, Hummers, and SUVs. Wall Street analysts are now questioning whether General Motors will survive into 2009. This type of loss in value has never occurred with real estate. Have you ever heard of someone losing 80 to 100 percent of their real estate value overnight? I sure haven't.

Another huge advantage of real estate over stocks and other investments is that you can take action to increase the value of the property. It is amazing the value increase you can experience by purchasing the worst house on the block and merely cutting back overgrown landscaping and painting the home. You can literally purchase a home for $85,000, paint it for $1,200, and increase its value to $95,000.

Commercial property values can also be enhanced by merely increasing the rents. For instance, if you purchase a commercial property, provide cosmetic improvements, and divide larger spaces into smaller spaces that demand a higher per-square-foot rental rate, you can experience a huge increase in value. For example, assuming you purchase a 5,000-square-foot building that was commanding rents of $1.25 per-square-foot (PSF) per month and subdivide the space into smaller spaces with market rents of $1.67 PSF per month, assuming a 10 percent cap rate, the value increase would amount to $252,000 ([($1.67 - $1.27) x 12] x 5,000 sf /10 percent). I do not know of any investment other than real estate that will allow you to use your creativity and/or sweat equity to increase the value of your assets.

**8. Tax Advantages**—Because the government is very supportive of property rights and having individuals assist in providing decent, affordable housing for the nation's population, many tax advantages are available for real estate investors that are not available to investors in stocks and bonds. While the topic of tax regulations can be very complicated and detail oriented, if you are going to be a serious real estate investor and pursue the worry-fee retirement, at a minimum you must become acquainted with the tax laws. I strongly suggest that you bring on a CPA as part of your Wealth Team (to be discussed later) to assist in matters of taxation and estate planning. While it is not the purpose of this book to discuss tax regulations surrounding real estate investing, I want to discuss the two major tax advantages of real estate over stocks and other investments, mainly: 1) depreciation, and 2) the tax-free sale of real estate.

Depreciation—As I previously discussed in Section 3, "Real Estates Provides Monthly Income," real estate investors are able to offset real estate income with the use of depreciation. Depreciation allows you to depreciate the value of the property (excluding land value) over time. Depreciation does not cost you any money, and yet it can provide a tax loss to offset your income. There is no such corresponding offset for income received from stocks or bonds.

Tax-Free Sale of Real Estate—As of the date of this writing, the government allows individuals and/or couples to exclude from the sale of their principal residence $250,000 and $500,000, respectively, provided that they have lived in the home for two of the last five years. As such, if you and your spouse purchased a home for $200,000 in 2003 and have lived in the home for two of last five years and sell the home in 2008 for $600,000, you do not have to pay taxes on your $400,000 ($600,000 - $200,000) gain! Let's look at a real-life example of this tax benefit. Richard and Amy purchased their principal residence in Scottsdale, Arizona, in 2002 for $410,000. In 2004 they sold their house for $829,000, making a profit of $419,000 in just two years. As the result of the sale and the federal government's exclusion of the gain on their principal residence, Richard and Amy paid no taxes on their $419,000 profit! If this had been a stock rather than a home, they would have had to pay a 15-percent capital gain tax on the profit, or $62,850 ($419,000 x 15 percent). This is a huge tax benefit that we will discuss later in the book as a way to accelerate your purchase of real estate investments.

For more information related to tax advantages of real estate, I recommend Diane Kennedy's book, *Real Estate Tax Loopholes*. This book discusses complex topics in an easy-to-understand format. As always, I suggest that you consult with your tax adviser on tax issues, as tax advantages vary from individual to individual. If you don't have a CPA, I strongly suggest that you add one to your Wealth Team, as the payment and/or deferral of taxes can have huge implications for your investment returns, net worth, and estate planning.

**9. With Real Estate You Can Obtain Cash Without Selling and/ or Paying Taxes**—As your real estate portfolio appreciates in value, you may refinance the property and pull out cash without paying any taxes. Excluding the use of margin loans, if you want to pull money out of stocks, you have to sell the stock, which may trigger a taxable event. As long as you have owned the stock for over twelve months, the gain on the sale of stock will be taxed at your capital gain rate, which as of the date of this writing is a maximum of 15 percent. With real estate, provided the value of your property has increased, you may refinance your property and receive income tax free. For instance, let's say you purchased a home five years ago for $200,000, and now the property is worth $400,000. Assume further that the outstanding mortgage you obtained when you purchased the home is now $150,000, leaving you with equity in the home of $250,000 ($400,000 - $150,000). If you obtained a new 80-percent loan on the value of the home, or $320,000 ($400,000 x 80 percent), and paid off the remaining $150,000 mortgage, you would walk away from the closing table with a check for $170,000 ($320,000 - $150,000). All of this money would go to you tax free to be used to spend in your retirement or to purchase new investment properties. The ability to pull cash out of real estate assets without triggering a taxable event is not available with other types of investments.

**10. Real Estate is the Simplest and Easiest Way to Create a Huge Net Worth with Very Little Cash**—For the nine reasons previously discussed, real estate is the only investment vehicle available to all investors, regardless of means, that will increase in value, provide tax benefits, and generate a monthly income that will allow you to reach a worry- free retirement. As I mentioned earlier in book, I began my real estate investment career in a bad real estate market with no money and bad credit. At present, the value of our family's real estate holdings is in excess of $7 million with equity of over $4 million. If we can do it, so can you!

Second of all, investing in real estate is a lot of fun. There isn't any place my wife and I go in our business and personal travels where we don't explore the local real estate market and look for potential real estate investments. As of this writing, in addition to the rental properties my wife and I own in the Phoenix metropolitan area, we own rental and investment property in the White Mountains of Arizona, near the northeast entrance to Yellowstone Park in Montana, on the beach along the Sea of Cortez in Mexico, as well as in Sydney, Australia. What makes this even better is that every time we go to Montana, Mexico, or Australia, we can write off a portion of the trip as a business expense. This is another tax benefit that the government allows.

## Conclusion

As you can see, real estate is an investment that provides a myriad of advantages that stocks and bonds do not. The Real Estate Return Maximizers are the reason that if you want to have a worry-free retirement, real estate has to be at the core of your investment strategy. In my opinion, without owning at least two to five rental properties in addition to your principal residence, you will not generate the returns, yields, net worth, and ongoing monthly income that will be necessary to support your retirement. As such, you may be forced to sell stocks, bonds, and mutual funds to provide for monthly living expenses, thus depleting your net worth and triggering potential taxable events and forcing you to live below the standard the living to which you are currently accustomed.

You may be saying to yourself right now, "OK, I can see why real estate should be included in my investment portfolio. However, how do I evaluate a potential real estate transaction, and how can I determine if I am on track to achieving my worry-free retirement?" Keep reading for the answer, as we'll discuss in the next chapter how you can achieve these goals.

# Chapter 7

## Making Real Estate Analysis Simple and Easy

*The Property Ledger*

Once my wife and I had acquired three investment properties, we began having challenges keeping track of the growth of our real estate portfolio and determining the financial results of our efforts. As real estate is the cornerstone of our investment strategy, this information was extremely important to us. I began to look for a software package that would not only let us evaluate individual real estate opportunities but would also provide information related to: 1) the value of our real estate portfolio when we retired, 2) the net monthly cash flow we might expect once the mortgages were paid off, as well as 3) various financial calculations related to each individual project and our real estate portfolio as a whole. After an exhaustive search, I could not locate such a software program. All of the software packages I found would only do very basic and limited financial calculations for one property. They did not provide the necessary sophisticated analysis that we required to not only provide the basic analysis when evaluating a property for acquisition, but one that also projected the long-term returns of our real estate portfolio as a whole. I thought that if we were facing this challenge, perhaps other real estate investors might have the same need for this information. As a result, I set out to develop an easy-to-use software program to satisfy our need for this information. Thus, The Property Ledger was born.

The Property Ledger is a web-based real estate software program that cannot only be utilized for the financial analysis of potential real estate acquisitions (single-family homes, condominiums, apartments, commercial buildings, mobile home parks, land, etc.) but will also track the financial returns of your entire real estate portfolio over time. The Property Ledger also features the Financial Dashboard for each project as well as your portfolio as a whole. The Financial Dashboard provides information related to: 1) the date at which the mortgage will be paid off, 2) the estimated equity you will have in the property as of the pay-off date, as well as 3) the net monthly cash flow that you can anticipate once the mortgage has been paid off. This is important information to have when you are attempting to estimate the net cash flow that you will have to live on during retirement.

Other features of The Property Ledger include:

- **The Electronic Library**—Allows you to scan and store purchase agreements, lease agreements, property management agreements, purchase documents, photos, and financial document related to each of your rental properties (Note: The Property Ledger utilizes a secured website to safeguard your information)

- **The Mortgage Wizard**—Allows you to finance and/or refinance a property with a multiple number of loans during an unlimited analysis time period. You can employ the use of fixed rate, adjustable rate, or interest-only loans. You also have the ability to utilize multiple loans to purchase investment properties, such as an 80-percent first mortgage and 10-percent second mortgage

- **The Financial Analyst**—Provides annual pre-tax and after-tax cash-flow projections for individual properties as well your portfolio as a whole. The financial analyst calculates the following annual financial ratios in relation to single-investment properties as well as your entire real estate portfolio: cash-on-cash return (COC), internal rate of return (IRR), net present value (NPV), debt service coverage (DSC) ratios, loan-to-value ratio (LTV), capitalization rates, as well as the gross rent multiplier (GRM).

- **The Report Writer**—Allows for the preparation of professional financial reports for all of your reporting needs, including 1) acquisition summary report (utilized for obtaining financing from banks and/or partners), partnership report (illustrates return to partners), 2) property cash flow (illustrates returns on property from rental operations, sale and/or appreciation of property as well as tax benefits), 3) rent roll (provides gross rents by tenant for multi-family or commercial buildings), 4) operating analysis (provides detailed information related to operating expenses in total and as a percentage of rental income as well as on a per-square-foot basis), 5) operating tax analysis (illustrates annual tax consequences of the investment property), 6) amortization schedules (provides a month-by-month amortization table for each loan related to your investment properties), 7) graph and charts (provides graphs and charts related to property financial performance).

- **Other Functions**—The Property Ledger will also allow you to access important analytical information:

    - Replace yearly estimates with actual operating results for each individual property in order to determine actual financial returns on property investments;
    - Input the acquisition of real estate investments on the date on which they occurred, including going back in time (i.e., July 24, 1994) and projecting forward. In this way, one is able to measure the performance of a single real estate investment or the entire real estate portfolio through the current time period as well as into the future.
    - Calculate before-tax and after-tax returns
    - Utilize general or very detailed assumptions for each property

The program is intuitive and easy to use, all information is safeguarded by bank-level security systems and is password-protected so that only you have access to the data, and all of your information is backed up nightly.

You can neither make informed decisions related to purchasing real estate investments nor chart the course of your worry-free retirement without performing financial due diligence. It is my opinion that The Property Ledger is the best real estate investment software available for individual real estate investors. I would like to provide you with a free two-month subscription to The Property Ledger as a way of saying thank you for allowing me to share the worry-free retirement plan with you and as a way for you to test and evaluate The Property Ledger. Given the power of The Property Ledge, I strongly suggest that it become the keystone to your Retirement Cash-Flow Solution.

In order to access your free two-month trial subscription to The Property Ledger go to the free offer section located at the back of the book and follow the directions to see how the The Property Ledger can be utilized to help chart your course to a worry-free retirement.

# Chapter 8

## The Property Ledger

In order to illustrate how The Property Ledger can be utilized to track your Retirement Cash-Flow Solution, I have prepared an example of a real estate portfolio as tracked utilizing The Property Ledger.

As the analysis of real estate acquisitions involves a number of assumptions related to rental income, monthly operating expenses, repairs and maintenance, financing, appreciation rates, as well as rental rate increases and operating expense escalations, it is imperative that you utilize a financial program to determine if the proposed property acquisition meets your investment criteria. The problem that I saw with existing real estate investment software was that all of the software programs had flaws:

1. They were Excel based.
2. They were not updated for updates in the tax code.
3. They did not allow for multiple loans to acquire property (i.e., first and second mortgages).
4. They did not allow for both default assumptions and specific assumptions for specific years.
5. They did not allow for refinancing during the analysis period of the property.

6. They only showed a twenty-year analysis period.

7. They only allowed the analysis of one property at a time.

8. They did not allow for various types of investments, including single-family homes, duplexes, apartments, office buildings, retail buildings, mobile home parks, land, etc.

9. They did not track the investment performance of all of my real estate holdings.

10. They provided no information on cash flow of my entire real estate portfolio.

11. They could not be accessed via the web.

12. They did not store any of my property records.

13. They were confusing and difficult to use.

In order to address all of the shortcomings listed above and have the ability to access my property records from anywhere in the world, I developed The Property Ledger. In order to give you a better understanding of the capabilities of The Property Ledger, I have illustrated some of the screen shots and reports below.

## Portfolio Summary

The screen shot below illustrates the summary page of The Property Ledger. As you can see, all of the individual's property holdings are illustrated along with the results of his or her respective rental activity, property sale/appreciation, cash position, and various investments return metrics. The Financial Dashboard provides an estimate as to when the last mortgage of the investment portfolio will be paid off, the net value of the portfolio, as well as what the portfolio's estimated monthly net cash flow will be at that point in time. This is important information, as this is the amount of money that the Retirement

Cash-Flow Solution will be generating that will be available for monthly living expenses or other pursuits.

Investor, LLC — Financial Dashboard

Number of Properties in Portfolio 2
Date of First Property Purchase 02/01/2001

Last Mortgage Pay-Off Date 02/01/2032
Equity of Portfolio at Pay-Off $1,198,110
Net Monthly Cashflow at Pay-Off $757 ($9,087 / 12)

Electronic Library

🔖 Retirement Vision   🔖 R.E. Navigator Forms

| Rental Operations | 2001 | 2002 | 2003 | 2004 | 2005 | 2006 | 2007 |
|---|---|---|---|---|---|---|---|
| Anthem, LLC | $1,374 | $1,912 | $1,670 | $1,535 | $1,682 | $1,404 | ($1,839) |
| Emerald, LLC | -- | $995 | $1,280 | $1,434 | $1,592 | $1,754 | ($544) |
| Total | $1,374 | $2,907 | $2,949 | $2,969 | $3,274 | $3,158 | ($2,383) |

| Property Sale | 2001 | 2002 | 2003 | 2004 | 2005 | 2006 | 2007 |
|---|---|---|---|---|---|---|---|
| Anthem, LLC | $19,058 | $30,985 | $44,698 | $64,217 | $86,863 | $107,825 | $117,914 |
| Emerald, LLC | -- | $20,661 | $33,117 | $48,257 | $69,436 | $93,843 | $106,070 |
| Total | $19,058 | $51,646 | $77,815 | $112,473 | $156,299 | $201,668 | $223,983 |

| Cash Position | 2001 | 2002 | 2003 | 2004 | 2005 | 2006 | 2007 |
|---|---|---|---|---|---|---|---|
| Anthem, LLC | $6,807 | $20,646 | $36,028 | $57,082 | $81,410 | $103,776 | $112,025 |
| Emerald, LLC | -- | $6,940 | $20,677 | $37,251 | $60,023 | $86,183 | $97,867 |
| Total | $6,807 | $27,587 | $56,705 | $94,332 | $141,432 | $189,960 | $209,892 |

| Return on Equity | 2001 | 2002 | 2003 | 2004 | 2005 | 2006 | 2007 |
|---|---|---|---|---|---|---|---|
| Anthem, LLC | 49.96% | 67.73% | 44.88% | 42.40% | 34.41% | 23.54% | 7.03% |
| Emerald, LLC | -- | 47.17% | 63.43% | 46.83% | 43.82% | 35.00% | 11.58% |
| Average | 49.96% | 57.45% | 54.16% | 44.61% | 39.11% | 29.27% | 9.30% |

| Cash-on-Cash Return on Investment | 2001 | 2002 | 2003 | 2004 | 2005 | 2006 | 2007 |
|---|---|---|---|---|---|---|---|
| Anthem, LLC | 49.96% | 151.53% | 264.43% | 418.95% | 597.50% | 761.66% | 822.20% |
| Emerald, LLC | -- | 47.17% | 140.52% | 253.15% | 407.90% | 585.68% | 647.24% |
| Average | 49.96% | 99.35% | 202.48% | 336.05% | 502.70% | 673.67% | 734.72% |

| Cash-on-Cash Return Before Taxes | 2001 | 2002 | 2003 | 2004 | 2005 | 2006 | 2007 |
|---|---|---|---|---|---|---|---|
| Anthem, LLC | -6.33% | -2.40% | -0.39% | 1.68% | 3.82% | 6.03% | -28.24% |
| Emerald, LLC | -- | -4.00% | 3.03% | 5.27% | 7.57% | 9.95% | -4.58% |
| Average | -6.33% | -3.20% | 1.32% | 3.47% | 5.70% | 7.99% | -16.41% |

| Cash-on-Cash Return After Taxes | 2001 | 2002 | 2003 | 2004 | 2005 | 2006 | 2007 |
|---|---|---|---|---|---|---|---|
| Anthem, LLC | 10.09% | 14.03% | 12.25% | 11.26% | 12.34% | 10.30% | -13.50% |
| Emerald, LLC | -- | 6.76% | 8.70% | 9.75% | 10.82% | 11.92% | -3.70% |
| Average | 10.09% | 10.39% | 10.47% | 10.50% | 11.58% | 11.11% | -8.60% |

| Internal Rate of Return | 2001 | 2002 | 2003 | 2004 | 2005 | 2006 | 2007 |
|---|---|---|---|---|---|---|---|
| Anthem, LLC | 49% | 60% | 57% | 54% | 51% | 47% | 41% |
| Emerald, LLC | -- | 47% | 56% | 54% | 52% | 49% | 43% |
| Average | 49.00% | 53.50% | 56.50% | 54.00% | 51.50% | 48.00% | 42.00% |

## *Individual Project Summary*

Each individual rental property has a summary page related to that property's rental activity, property sale/appreciation, cash position, and various investment returns metrics. Selected data from the individual project summary automatically flows to the portfolio summary.

**Property** Emerald, LLC
**Address** 5382 N. Emerald Creek Drive
**City, State** Florence, AZ
**County** USA
**Purchase Date** 02/01/2002
**Purchase Price** $135,000

**Financial Dashboard**
**Mortgage Pay-Off Date** 02/01/2032
**Net Equity at Pay-Off** $584,115
**Net Monthly Cashflow at Pay-Off** $543 ($6,521 / 12)

Electronic Library
 Lease  Project Photos  Wealth Team Contacts

Financial Analyst™

| Rental Operations | 2002 | 2003 | 2004 | 2005 | 2006 | 2007 | 2008 |
|---|---|---|---|---|---|---|---|
| Rental Income | $11,500 | $14,214 | $14,640 | $15,080 | $15,532 | $15,998 | $16,478 |
| Other Income | $0 | $0 | $0 | $0 | $0 | $0 | $0 |
| Vacancy & Credits | ($345) | ($426) | ($439) | ($452) | ($466) | ($480) | ($494) |
| Operating Expenses | ($4,170) | ($4,253) | ($4,338) | ($4,425) | ($4,514) | ($4,604) | ($4,696) |
| **Net Operating Income** | **$6,985** | **$9,534** | **$9,863** | **$10,202** | **$10,552** | **$10,914** | **$11,287** |
| Mortgage Payments | ($7,573) | ($9,088) | ($9,088) | ($9,088) | ($9,088) | ($9,088) | ($9,088) |
| Capital Improvements | $0 | $0 | $0 | $0 | $0 | ($2,500) | $0 |
| Operating Income Taxes: Benefit / ( Expense ) | $1,583 | $833 | $659 | $478 | $290 | $130 | ($73) |
| **Net Cash Flow from Rental Operations** | **$995** | **$1,280** | **$1,434** | **$1,592** | **$1,754** | **($544)** | **$2,127** |
| **Property Sales / Appreciation** | | | | | | | |
| Projected Sale Price - Original Cost | $154,000 | $170,940 | $191,453 | $220,171 | $253,196 | $265,856 | $279,149 |
| Projected Sale Price - Improvements | $0 | $0 | $0 | $0 | $0 | $2,625 | $2,756 |
| Selling Expenses | ($9,240) | ($10,256) | ($11,487) | ($13,210) | ($15,192) | ($16,109) | ($16,914) |
| **Adjusted Projected Sales Price** | **$144,760** | **$160,684** | **$179,966** | **$206,960** | **$238,005** | **$252,372** | **$264,991** |
| First Mortgage Balance Payoff | ($98,982) | ($97,691) | ($96,321) | ($94,866) | ($93,321) | ($91,681) | ($89,940) |
| Second Mortgage Balance Payoff | ($21,351) | ($21,159) | ($20,951) | ($20,726) | ($20,483) | ($20,218) | ($19,932) |
| Tax Benefit - Suspended Loss | $0 | $0 | $0 | $0 | $0 | $0 | $0 |
| Income Taxes from Sale: Benefit / ( Expense ) | ($3,766) | ($8,716) | ($14,437) | ($21,932) | ($30,358) | ($34,403) | ($38,622) |
| **Net Cash Flow from Property Sale** | **$20,661** | **$33,117** | **$48,257** | **$69,436** | **$93,843** | **$106,070** | **$116,497** |
| **Cash / Equity Position** | | | | | | | |
| Net Cash Generated this Year | $995 | $1,280 | $1,434 | $1,592 | $1,754 | ($544) | $2,127 |
| Net Cumulative Cash Generated | $0 | $995 | $2,275 | $3,709 | $5,301 | $7,056 | $6,512 |
| Net Cash Generated - Property Sale | $20,661 | $33,117 | $48,257 | $69,436 | $93,843 | $106,070 | $116,497 |
| Cash Inflow (Outflow) from Refinancing | $0 | $0 | $0 | $0 | $0 | $0 | $0 |
| Original Initial Investment | ($14,715) | ($14,715) | ($14,715) | ($14,715) | ($14,715) | ($14,715) | ($14,715) |
| **Total Net Cumulative Cash Generated** | **$6,940** | **$20,677** | **$37,251** | **$60,023** | **$86,193** | **$97,867** | **$110,421** |
| **Financial Analysis** | | | | | | | |
| Debt Service Coverage | 0.92 | 1.05 | 1.09 | 1.12 | 1.16 | 1.20 | 1.24 |
| Loan to Value | 78.14% | 69.53% | 61.25% | 52.50% | 44.95% | 42.09% | 39.36% |
| Cap Rate based on FMV | 4.54% | 5.58% | 5.15% | 4.63% | 4.17% | 4.07% | 4.00% |
| Gross Rent Multiplier ( year ) | 13.39 | 12.03 | 13.08 | 14.60 | 16.30 | 16.62 | 16.94 |
| Net Present Value, 10.00% | 4,972 | 14,617 | 24,581 | 36,838 | 48,771 | 50,068 | 51,068 |
| Return on Equity | 47.17% | 63.43% | 46.83% | 43.82% | 35.00% | 11.58% | 11.15% |
| Cash-on-cash return on investment | 47.17% | 140.52% | 253.15% | 407.90% | 585.68% | 647.24% | 731.67% |
| Cash-on-cash return - before taxes | -4.00% | 3.03% | 5.27% | 7.57% | 9.95% | -4.58% | 14.95% |
| Cash-on-cash return - after taxes | 6.76% | 8.70% | 9.75% | 10.82% | 11.92% | -3.70% | 14.46% |
| Internal Rate of Return | 47% | 56% | 54% | 52% | 49% | 43% | 38% |

## *Project Inputs*

Assumptions related to the purchase of the property, financing, revenues, expenses, taxes, and partnership information are easily entered into the data input pages. An example of the typical input page is illustrated below. As you can see, the data input pages include the instructions related to each input, and the program has been developed such that it will notify you if your assumptions are in conflict with other assumptions.

---

**Property Value Info**

**General Values**

**Date of Purchase**
02/01/2002 ▦ — Insert date of property purchase.

**Purchase Price of Property**
$135,000 — Insert purchase price of property.

**Current FMV of Property**
$140,000 — Insert fair market value (FMV) of property **only if FMV is different from the purchase price**. Appreciation will be based upon Purchase Price unless current FMV is inserted.

**Five Year Personal Property**
$0 — Personal property included in purchase price to be depreciated over 5 years.

**Seven Year Personal Property**
$0 — Personal property included in purchase price to be depreciated over 7 years.

**% of Cost Allocated to Land**
20.00% — Value of land expressed as a percentage of purchase price. Usually around 20%.

**Default Annual Property Appreciation Rate**
5.00% — Insert default annual appreciation rate of property. This rate will be utilized unless variable property appreciation rates are utilized.

**Variable Property Appreciation Rates**
**Enter Rates**

# Reports

The Property Ledger allows you to generate professional-looking reports to be used for your own reporting needs or those of your bank and/or partners. An example of a tax analysis report is illustrated below.

Tax Analysis

| Rental Operations Analysis | 2002 | 2003 | 2004 | 2005 | 2006 | 2007 | 2008 |
|---|---|---|---|---|---|---|---|
| Net Operating Income | $6,985 | $9,534 | $9,863 | $10,202 | $10,552 | $10,914 | $11,287 |
| Depreciation for Tax Purposes | ($3,764) | ($3,927) | ($3,927) | ($3,927) | ($3,927) | ($4,014) | ($4,018) |
| Points Amortization | (39) | (42) | (42) | (42) | (42) | (42) | (42) |
| Interest Expenses - First Mortgage | ($5,472) | ($5,897) | ($5,817) | ($5,732) | ($5,642) | ($5,546) | ($5,445) |
| Interest Expenses - Second Mortgage | ($1,571) | ($1,700) | ($1,684) | ($1,666) | ($1,648) | ($1,627) | ($1,605) |
| Interest Expenses - Refinance | -- | -- | -- | -- | -- | -- | -- |
| **Taxable Income from Operations** | **($3,861)** | **($2,033)** | **($1,608)** | **($1,166)** | **($707)** | **($316)** | **$177** |
| Federal & State Tax Rate | 41.00% | 41.00% | 41.00% | 41.00% | 41.00% | 41.00% | 41.00% |
| **Tax Benefit / (Expense) from Operations** | **$1,583** | **$833** | **$659** | **$478** | **$290** | **$130** | **($73)** |
| **Property Sale Analysis** | | | | | | | |
| Net Projected Sales Price | $144,760 | $160,684 | $179,966 | $206,960 | $238,005 | $252,372 | $264,991 |
| Original Cost of Property | ($135,000) | ($135,000) | ($135,000) | ($135,000) | ($135,000) | ($135,000) | ($135,000) |
| Property Improvements | $0 | $0 | $0 | $0 | $0 | ($2,500) | ($2,500) |
| Points Paid | ($1,215) | ($1,215) | ($1,215) | ($1,215) | ($1,215) | ($1,215) | ($1,215) |
| **Gain (Loss) on Property Sale** | **$8,545** | **$24,469** | **$43,751** | **$70,745** | **$101,790** | **$113,657** | **$126,276** |
| Accumulated Depreciation / Amortization | $3,802 | $7,772 | $11,741 | $15,711 | $19,680 | $23,737 | $27,797 |
| **Taxable Gain (Loss) on Property Sale** | **$12,347** | **$32,241** | **$55,492** | **$86,456** | **$121,470** | **$137,394** | **$154,073** |
| Capital Gain & State Tax Rate on Sale | 23.00% | 23.00% | 23.00% | 23.00% | 23.00% | 23.00% | 23.00% |
| Income Tax Benefit / (Expense) | ($3,390) | ($7,947) | ($13,275) | ($20,377) | ($28,411) | ($32,054) | ($35,871) |
| Recapture Tax | ($376) | ($769) | ($1,162) | ($1,555) | ($1,947) | ($2,349) | ($2,751) |
| **Total Tax Benefit / (Expense) from Sale** | **($3,766)** | **($8,716)** | **($14,437)** | **($21,932)** | **($30,358)** | **($34,403)** | **($38,622)** |

If you are serious about tracking your progress toward your Retirement Cash-Flow Solution, I strongly suggest that you employ the use of The Property Ledger, as it is the only real estate analytical tool that I am aware of that will provide you with a yardstick for measuring your progress toward your worry-free retirement. Not using The Property Ledger would be similar to attempting to drive from New York to Los Angeles without a roadmap. Once again, I urge you to take advantage of the free offer included at the back of this book to register today for your free two-month test trial of The Property Ledger.

# Chapter 9

## Pull Back the Curtain
## on Real Estate Investing

*Real Estate Investing is a Business*

Unlike investing in the stock market, where you can purchase a stock or mutual fund and perhaps check on the financial performance of the stock or mutual fund every other month, investing in real estate is a business that will take your time and attention. If you are to be a successful real estate investor, you should be prepared to treat investing in real estate as a full-time occupation. By a full-time occupation, I do not mean an occupation in which you have to show up to work each day, but rather an occupation in which you are continually engaged in looking for the next potential deal as you go about your day. I want to make it clear that investing in real estate is not a way to get rich quick. If it were, everyone would be doing it. You must be mentally, emotionally, and physically prepared and willing to spend some time to achieve the goals of your worry-free retirement.

When you first start out in your real estate investing career, I recommend that you get involved in all aspects of the property management, including marketing, leasing, repairs, maintenance, and record keeping, in order to get on-the-job training in relation to business of real estate management.

Once you have acquired two or three rental properties, however, you will have had all of the on-the-job training that is necessary, and your unique skills and abilities will be better served in finding more rental properties to add to your portfolio. At this point in your investment career, I suggest that you begin to assemble your Wealth Team.

### Creating Your Wealth Team

The purpose of the Wealth Team is to generate leverage for you. This is not leverage in the monetary sense, but rather leverage in the sense of time. By creating your Wealth Team, you will be able to leverage your time by having your Wealth Team do much of the work you had been doing, allowing you to look for additional real estate investments or enjoy other pursuits.

While everyone's Wealth Team may differ based upon the requirements of the particular investor, at a minimum I suggest the following professionals be considered as part of your Wealth Team as illustrated in the figure below.

The Wealth Team

*The Property Ledger*—The Property Ledger is the foundation of the Real Estate Wealth-Building System as well as the Retirement Cash-Flow Solution and should be the cornerstone of your Wealth Team. The Property Ledger functions as the nerve center of your Retirement Cash-Flow Solution and is the tool that is utilized to prepare the acquisition analysis required for evaluating rental property acquisitions, preparing financing requests, monitoring the growth of your net worth, calculating your investment returns, and projecting your properties' and your portfolio's cash flow.

*Real Estate Agent*—The purpose of the real estate agent is to continually search for real estate investments for you that meet your investment criteria. Not only can a real estate agent locate the next investment property, but he or she can also prepare market comparables for both sales and rental rates and assemble statistics related to the market. The information generated by the real estate agent can then be input into The Property Ledger to evaluate the financial merits of the investment opportunity.

*Property Manager*—A great property manager can save you a lot of time and money. Property managers not only lease the property once it has been acquired, but they also perform routine maintenance on the property, clean the unit, clean the carpets, paint the walls, and ready the property for rental upon the departure of a tenant. Charges for property managers are dependent upon the tasks that they are asked to perform, so it is crucial that you understand what your needs are in relation to the property management function and communicate such needs to the property management company when you are interviewing property managers for your Wealth Team. Don't be afraid to ask the property manager for a customized set of services tailor made to fit your requirements. As an example, because I have a great handyman whom I found when I was acting as the property manager, and because my handyman was cheaper than my property manager's handyman, I asked that the property manager not use his handyman, but rather use mine for any repairs on my units.

*Mortgage Broker/Banker*—The mortgage broker and/or banker is one of the most important individuals on the Wealth Team. By keeping all of our personal and financial information with one individual whom I keep updated every quarter, I am able to call the mortgage broker with the particulars of a transaction and he takes it from there, preparing the loan package and coordinating information with the real estate broker and the title company. I do not have to do anything related to obtaining a mortgage or coordinating the closing, and this saves me a huge amount of time.

*CPA/Tax Specialist*—One of the major benefits of real estate investing is tax benefits. In order to take advantage of all of the tax advantages that accrue as a result of real estate investing and ownership, you will to need have a good CPA on your Wealth Team. I suggest a CPA who specializes in real estate and preferably one who is actively involved in real estate investing for his or her own portfolio. Make sure you listen to your CPA's advice and follow through on his or her recommendations. As you will own a number of rental properties as part of your Retirement Cash-Flow Solution, make sure that either you or your spouse qualifies as a real estate professional, so that you can enjoy all of the tax benefits of real estate ownership.

*Insurance Specialist*—Get a good insurance agent who can handle all of your insurance needs related to your rental properties as a member of your Wealth Team. The ideal insurance specialist will balance your insurance coverage needs with your property's cash-flow requirements.

*Attorney*—It is good to have a relationship with an attorney you can turn to when required. Obviously, you want the attorney to be a specialist in real estate to assist with tenant issues, liability issues, and tax issues.

*Bookkeeper*—Real estate investing is a business and should be treated as such. Hire a bookkeeper to track revenues and expenses for your portfolio and to coordinate with your CPA at tax time. I also have my bookkeeper assist in scanning records into The Property Ledger and provide actual operating results so that I can continually monitor my real estate portfolio's growth over time with The Property Ledger. If you do not wish to hire a bookkeeper, at a minimum I strongly suggest that your purchase an easy-to-use accounting software package such as QuickBooks in order to allow you to track your revenues and expenses as well as to prepare monthly and annual financial reports.

*Handyman*—I can't tell you how much time and money a good handyman can save you. In my case, not only does my handyman do work on behalf of my property management company, which saves me approximately 30 percent from what the property management company would charge, he knows all of my properties inside and out and knows exactly what has to be done to each one every time there is a tenant turnover.

## *Real Estate Investing is a Journey, Not a Destination*

When I talk about investing in real estate, I am not referring to purchasing properties and then flipping them to someone else in order to make a few thousand dollars. That is speculating, not investing. The type of real estate investing that will allow you to have a worry-free retirement relates to purchasing properties and renting the properties to create a steady stream of income to pay off the mortgages and generate excess cash that can be used for future investments, the creation of wealth, and/or paying for living expenses in retirement. You should treat your investment portfolio just as you would your 401(k), Roth IRA, or your IRA, meaning never touching the income or value generated by the rental properties unless it is to purchase additional rental properties. In this way, you can continue to compound your investment returns and generate a significant amount of wealth over time. From the beginning, I have stressed that the worry-free retirement is not a get-rich-quick scheme. It could take you twenty years to get to the point where you have the income and net worth levels that will allow you to retire and live in the style that you desire. However, what is wrong with waiting twenty years, if in the process you generate income on which to live that would not have been available to you? The number of years it will take you to get to your investment goal will be directly proportionate to the amount and time that you devote to real estate investing. If you invest the time and effort and are able to purchase two properties a year, you will arrive at your goal much faster than if you purchase only one property every other year.

The other aspect of real estate investing that I want to be up front with you about, is that it will take sacrifices on your part in both time and money. There will be times when you may want to go to a movie or watch TV rather than to prospect for more potential real estate deals, or you may want to take the $5,000 in cash for the next down payment on a rental property and use it for a vacation. I urge you to think about how you are using both your time and your money. When you look at the opportunity cost of not finding the next real estate deal or foregoing the next rental property for a vacation, think about how much wealth that the foregone transaction may have added to your net worth or how much extra monthly cash flow the rental unit may have added to your worry-free retirement. While I am not advocating that you not enjoy life or skip vacations, I am challenging you to live differently in the present so that you may live differently in the future.

Lastly, there will be times, such as now, when the real estate market is down. During these times, I urge you not to panic! Real estate is a cyclical business, meaning it goes up and down over specific time periods. However, ever since records have been kept on real estate appreciation, real estate has appreciated at an annual average rate of approximately 6 percent. There may be times when you see the values of your properties going down, and when this happens, I suggest that you do nothing. The only way to actually lose money in real estate is to sell. If you do not sell, you can't lose money, and as the purpose of the worry-free retirement is to generate wealth and monthly cash flow, stay the course and keep your properties rented and continue to pay down your mortgages. The value of your properties will go back up over time, and you will be in the black again. The beauty of real estate is that time cures all mistakes and/or changes in the market. In fact, when the real estate market declines, I suggest that this is the best time to look for deals, as sellers are more apt to work with you to structure little or no-money-down transactions.

### Continue Your Real Estate Education

Real estate investing is a journey, not a destination. Make the commitment to yourself to continually learn more about real estate investing, business, creative thinking, and finance while surrounding yourself with like-minded individuals. One recommendation is to join a real estate investment club in your area. Real estate clubs typically hold monthly meetings and discuss topics of interest to the real estate investor, such as financing ideas, short sales, value enhancement methods, market trends, landlord / tenant issues, and other matters relevant to that particular market. The clubs will also host ongoing educational and speaker events. One of the great things about investment clubs is that they allow you to associate on a monthly basis with individuals such as yourself who have decided to take their financial freedom seriously and are working hard to make it happen. Personally, I find making contact with like-minded individuals refreshing, as most of the time I am surrounded by pessimistic individuals who believe that they are victims of their fate and are unwilling to make changes in their lives to have a bigger future. You can find a real estate investment club in your area by going to www.reiclubs.com.

Additionally, continue to read books on the subject of real estate investing. I typically read up to four books a month on the subjects of business and real estate. Think about the knowledge you would have if rather than watching thirty minutes of TV in the evenings you read a book, with the goal of reading three books a month? In a year you would have read thirty-six books, and in ten years it would amount to 360 books. Do you think that reading 360 books would help you to develop as a better real estate investor and businessperson? You bet it would. Because my career forces me to travel a great deal, I listen to CDs in the car and download CDs onto my iPod so that as I travel I can listen to business books and motivational messages. This allows me to complete a fifth book per month while I am a captive in my car or on an airplane.

# Chapter 10

## Real Estate Investment Strategies

*Overview*

The first thing you have to remember is that the creation of the Retirement Cash-Flow Solution as well as your worry-free retirement will take time. It will not happen overnight, and you will have to take continued action over the months and years to achieve the goals you set for yourself.

The Retirement Cash-Flow Solution and worry-free retirement are investment philosophies. They are not money-making techniques where you buy property, fix up the property, and sell it for a profit, only to have to repeat the process again. The idea behind the worry-free retirement is to invest today's time and money into purchasing rental properties that will pay you and your extended family for the rest of your life as well as theirs. Sure, the quick profit may sound enticing. However, when you purchase property using the power of leverage and lease the property for enough money to cover the monthly operating expenses, every month when the tenants make their lease payments, they are making a contribution to your worry-free retirement. It may take a number of years before you are generating sufficient cash flow from rental activities before you can begin to pull money out of the properties on which to live. However, during this time you have enjoyed the power of leverage, seen the property appreciate, increased your net worth, and enjoyed the tax benefits of real estate. I guarantee you that if you can just cover your expenses when you purchase the property, over the years the trickle of money from the property will become a stream, and upon payoff of the mortgage, it will become a raging river. Remember, investing for the worry-free retirement takes patience, but I give you my guarantee that you will achieve your goals if you just take it one day at a time and put one foot in front of the other as you march toward your financial goals.

## *Investment Strategies for the Retirement Cash-Flow Solution*

The following represents my thoughts related to potential investment strategies for your real estate portfolio:

1. Purchase properties that will appeal to the largest target market—In order to have the strongest demand for the rental of your properties, I suggest that you purchase homes that will appeal to the greatest number of people. Generally, these are three-bedroom, two-bathroom homes with a garage and/ or carport located in middle-class neighborhoods ranging in size from 1,000 to 1,600 square feet.

2. Avoid urban fringes and purchase properties near employment and transportation nodes—Whether we want to accept it or not, we are now in a new world economic paradigm in which the chances for the price of a gallon of gas to decline substantially for an extended period of time are very slim. The new emerging economies of China and India and their people's desire for the trappings of the western middle class, including homes and cars, will lead to even more demands on fossil fuels and thus increase its price. As such, I strongly

recommend looking for rental properties that will continue to appreciate even if gas prices hit $7 per gallon. It is my opinion that we could see many homes that have been constructed on the fringes on major metropolitan areas decrease in value significantly as the price of gas increases and families have to spend more of their disposable income on fuel costs and increasingly expensive consumer goods as the result of increased manufacturing and transportation costs. For example, for every dollar increase in the price of a gallon of gas, the purchase price that an individual with a twenty-five-mile round trip commute is able to accommodate is decreased by approximately $5,000. The effect is doubled if both spouses must make similar commutes. I recommend looking for properties that are located closer to a city's urban center rather than the fringe, and that are also located near employment centers, mass transit stations, and/or other transportation nodes, such as freeways.

3. Purchase Properties Located in Excellent School Districts— As we move more and more toward an information, technology, and knowledge-based economy, the importance of education will continue to grow. As such, I strongly recommend that you purchase properties that are located in strong academic school districts. As your primary tenants will be families, typically with children, it will be important to purchase properties located in the best school districts. For example, a family located outside of an excellent school district will often pay from $300 to $400 per month, per child, for a private school. In the case of two children, this could cost approximately $800 per month. It stands to reason that if you have a rental property located in an excellent

school district you could get $200 more rent per month than you could get for a property located in a poor school district because the family does not have to send the children to a private school.

4. Utilize Fixed Mortgages To Purchase Property—When dealing with rental properties, the ability to predict your ongoing operating expenses is critical to the Retirement Cash-Flow Solution. Because of this, I recommend only using fixed-rate mortgages. It may be tempting to obtain an adjustable-rate mortgage in order to have a lower payment in the initial year or two after an acquisition. However, the interest rate on the loan will go up, and generally the adjustable-rate mortgage interest rates increase at a level that is higher than that of rental rates. Don't put yourself through the agony of worrying what next year's mortgage payment will be. Lock in the lowest possible interest rate at the time of the acquisition with a fixed-rate mortgage so that you can determine with certainty what your mortgage payments will be for the remaining term of the loan.

5. Consider fifteen-year mortgages rather than thirty-year mortgages—Whenever possible, I strongly suggest that you consider the use of fifteen-year mortgages rather than thirty-year mortgages. With the exception of four of our rental properties, all of our family's properties are on fifteen-year mortgages. Our reason for having fifteen-year mortgages is that we want to pay –them off as quickly as possible with the least amount of money to get to our worry-free retirement vision. I have prepared the table below to summarize the differences in monthly costs and total payments over the life of a fifteen-year and thirty-year mortgage for the

acquisition of a $240,000 property assuming a 10-percent down payment.

| Comparison of 15 Year vs. 30 Year Mortgages | | | |
|---|---|---|---|
| Description | (A)<br>15 Year | (B)<br>30 Year | (A) - (B)<br>Difference |
| Home Price | $240,000 | $240,000 | - |
| Down Payment Percentage | 10% | 10% | - |
| Total Down Payment | $24,000 | $24,000 | - |
| Loan Amount | $216,000 | $216,000 | - |
| Interest Rate | 6.00% | 6.50% | -0.50% |
| Term of Mortgage (Years) | 15 | 30 | (15) |
| Annual Payment | $22,240 | $16,541 | $5,699 |
| Monthly Payment | $1,853 | $1,378 | $475 |
| Total Payment Over Life of Loan | $333,599 | $496,222 | ($162,622) |

The benefits of the fifteen-year mortgage versus the thirty-year mortgage are huge. Not only is the interest rate for a fifteen-year mortgage lower than that of a thirty-year mortgage, but because you are paying the principal back at a faster rate, the savings you will enjoy between the two mortgages can be staggering. In the example above, by paying an additional $475 per month with the fifteen-year mortgage, you will save $162,622 in interest payments that can be used to fund other rental properties or to pay down mortgages on other existing rental properties. Paying an additional $475 in the early years of a rental property acquisition may cause you to have a negative cash flow on the property, but if your finances allow paying the additional shortfall, you may want to consider paying the difference. Consider the additional payment to be a forced savings program, as the additional money that you are paying is increasing your equity in the property by paying down the outstanding principal balance on the mortgage.

A derivation of this strategy is to obtain a fixed-rate thirty-year mortgage and make mortgage payments every two weeks. For example, by breaking up the $1,996 mortgage payment on a $300,000 property into two payments of $998 made every two weeks, you will pay off the thirty-year mortgage in twenty-three years rather than thirty years and save approximately $106,000 in interest payments. The one drawback to this approach versus the fifteen-year mortgage is that when individuals enter into the bi-monthly payment plans, they typically do not follow through on the payments because some other need for the funds comes up, such as a new car or a dream vacation. The easier way is to just get a fixed-rate fifteen-year mortgage and stick with it.

6. Buy and Hold Strategy/Never Sell Properties—It has always been our strategy to purchase rental properties at an attractive price and to hold those properties for the long term with no thought of selling the property. We do this for a number of reasons:

   o Selling rental properties takes us off course from our worry-free retirement vision of having twenty homes debt free, generating $40,000 (twenty homes x $2,000 average monthly rent) in gross income per month.

   o To sell a rental property after it has appreciated requires me to find another property containing the same value attributes as the property that was sold. If we do this through a tax-free 1031 exchange (Starker Exchange) in which we are not taxed for the profit we have made on the house, we only have forty-five days to identify a property or properties to acquire to replace the property being sold. This can open us up to hasty and foolish decisions.

o   By selling homes we incur transaction costs such as potential tax consequences, brokerage commissions, financing charges, and closing costs that diminish our capital and our ultimate investment returns.

Over the years, I have seen many investors purchase and sell rental properties for short-term gains and have always thought of them as speculators and not investors. My thoughts mirror those of Warren Buffet, who jokes that calling someone who trades actively in the market an investor "is like calling someone who repeatedly engages in one-night stands a romantic." My real estate investment mentality more closely aligns with that of Mark Twain, who said, "Put all of your eggs in one basket—and watch that basket." In our case, other than the consulting practice, we have the largest component of our family's net worth invested in real estate that we intend to hold for the rest of our lives and pass on to our children.

# Chapter 11

## Financing Strategies
## To Acquire Real Estate

The most common complaint I come across in relation to investing in real estate is either "I have horrible credit and can't get a loan," or "I don't have any money to invest in real estate." The first thing you have to do is to remove the word can't from your vocabulary and come to accept the fact that if you do not take care of your financial destiny, no one, including the government, will do it for you. When I started investing in real estate, I could have used both of the statements above. However, I decided that even though I had horrible credit and no money, I was going to use my mind and work hard to begin my real estate portfolio. If I did it, so can you.

*Strategies to Get Started Purchasing Real Estate*
There is a multitude of ways to finance the purchase of real estate in addition to the traditional method of paying 10 to 20 percent of the purchase price down and obtaining a first mortgage from a lending institution for the balance. While this is oftentimes the most efficient means of completing a transaction, in some instances an investor may not have the necessary capital for the 10- to 20-percent down payment or they may have poor or nonexistent credit.

In light of this, I will discuss a number of financing methods that may be utilized to acquire property with very little money down. Regardless of your means, you should always attempt to purchase property with as small an investment as possible as you will dramatically increase your rate of return by doing so. As such, even though you may have huge cash reserves with which to purchase rental properties, to the extent that you employ the Real Estate Return Maximizers and the power of leverage, your returns will be magnified and your wealth dramatically accelerated.

When I started out investing in real estate, I utilized a number of these techniques, not so much out of a desire to enhance my returns, but because it was the only way I could purchase property given my financial situation. Remember, the secret to wealth creation is leverage. The less of your money that you utilize in a transaction and the more of OPM utilized in the acquisition of real estate, the faster you will achieve your worry-free retirement.

The following financing techniques are described in detail so you may employ them immediately in the acquisition of property. When I started investing in real estate, the real estate market was in turmoil as the result of the savings and loan meltdown with conditions very similar to those currently being experienced as the result of overbuilding, speculation, and lax lending standards. In my mind, this is the perfect time to employ some of the techniques outlined below, because when sellers are having a difficult time selling their properties, they are very open to the techniques outlined below.

## Creative Financing Techniques

### Technique Number 1
**Obtain a new mortgage and have the seller carry back a second mortgage**

Technique number 1 works well when the seller has substantial equity in the property and is willing to work with you to reach a sale. This is the technique that I utilized to start my real estate investment portfolio in the mid-1990s.

Assume that a seller of a $200,000 home has a $100,000 first mortgage on the property and is seeking $30,000 in cash from you and is willing to carry back a second mortgage in the amount of $70,000 ($200,000 less $100,000 first mortgage less $30,000 cash payment). As such, you would obtain a new 65- percent first mortgage of $130,000 ($200,000 x 65 percent). You would pay off the existing $100,000 mortgage and pay the seller his $30,000 cash. You would then give the seller a second mortgage of $70,000.

In structuring the terms of the second mortgage, I suggest that you attempt to get an interest-only loan at a fixed rate for the longest term possible. Typically, sellers will agree to five-to-seven-year terms with a balloon payment at the end of the period. Have the seller allow you to prepay the second mortgage at any time with no prepayment penalty. This way, as the property appreciates in value, you can refinance the property with a new first mortgage, paying off both the initial first mortgage as well as the seller's second mortgage.

### Technique Number 2
**Wrap-around mortgage**

Technique Number 2 involves giving the seller of property a wrap-around mortgage (wrap mortgage) note rather than cash. Under the terms of a wrap mortgage, the seller's existing first mortgage remains in place, and the seller remains as the titleholder and continues to make payments on the underlying existing mortgage with payments received from the new buyer under the terms of the wrap mortgage. Once the underlying first mortgage is paid off, the wrap mortgage, which was in second position, moves up to first position automatically.

For example, a seller acquired a property ten years ago for $125,000 with a 10-percent down payment with a loan of $112,500 at 7 percent interest for twenty-five years with a monthly payment of $795.13.

You purchase the property at the end of year ten for $200,000 with no money down, offering a wrap mortgage of $200,000 at 8.25 percent interest for 30 years with monthly payments of $1,502.

At the time of the sale, the seller's remaining balance on the existing first mortgage is $88,462, indicating equity of $111,538 ($200,000 - $88,462). When the first mortgage is paid off in fifteen (twenty-five less ten) years, the remaining principal on the balance of the $200,000 wrap note will be $154,822. Therefore, the seller's equity has increased from $111,538 to $154,822, or 38 percent. This is one of the reasons that the seller may consider the use of a wrap mortgage.

At the close of the sale, you would make payments of $1,502 to the seller (or better yet a trustee), who would then remit a payment of $795 to the holder of the first mortgage. After fifteen years when the first mortgage is paid off, the property is deeded to you subject to the wrap mortgage.

## *Technique Number 3*
### Sale of principal residence—
### Purchase new home and reinvest remaining proceeds

Under this scenario, it is assumed that you have a principal residence that you have lived in for two of the last five years. It is further assumed that the adjusted basis of the property is $250,000, and that the property is currently valued at $750,000.

Using technique number 3, you would sell your principal residence for $750,000. The gain of $500,000 ($750,000 - $250,000) would be received tax free by you and your spouse (limitation of $250,000 for single individuals), and the $500,000 in sale proceeds received would be utilized to purchase a principal residence and to invest in additional rental properties. Let's assume that you use $250,000 to pay cash for a $250,000 three-bedroom, two-bathroom home and utilize the remaining $250,000 to purchase $2.5 million ($250,000 / 10 percent) in rental properties with 90-percent loans to continue to build your Retirement Cash-Flow Solution and your worry-free retirement.

## *Technique 4*
### Home-equity loan

A great source of capital for beginning investors can be found in your own home. Many lending institutions are happy to make loans of up to 90 percent of your home's value. The interest rates associated with home-equity loans are higher than first mortgages, as home-equity loans are in second position behind the first mortgage. Typically, a home-equity loan will have a term of between five and fifteen years. It should be noted that interest payments related to a second mortgage on your residence are tax deductible within certain limitations. Utilizing this financing technique, you would take a second mortgage on your principal residence and use the loan proceeds to purchase rental properties.

## *Technique 5*
## Lease /purchase option

You don't always have to purchase a property to enjoy the benefits of appreciation. One way to accomplish this is to enter into a lease/ purchase agreement with the landlord/seller of property. Under this scenario, you find a landlord/seller who is willing to enter into a lease/purchase agreement with you. At the time of this writing, I have seen hundreds of ads in the newspapers from sellers advertising that they are willing to enter into lease/purchase agreements. Under a lease/ purchase transaction, you agree to lease the home from the landlord/seller with the ability to purchase the home at some point in the future for a specific price. While you are renting the property from the landlord/seller, a percentage of your rent is going toward the down payment related to the purchase of the home. For example, assuming that a landlord/seller has a home that she is willing to enter into a lease/purchase agreement for a rental payment of $1,000 per month with $600 of each rental payment going toward the down payment if the tenant decides to exercise the purchase option at a future sales price of $150,000. Utilizing this technique, you would enter into a separate lease agreement with the landlord, laying out the terms of the lease. Make sure that as of part of the lease there is a clause that will allow you to sublease the home to a tenant of your choice. You then enter into a separate purchase agreement spelling out the terms of the purchase and the amount of lease payment being credited toward the down payment. Once the paperwork has been signed, you advertise for a tenant to lease the property from you for $1,000 per month. Assuming that you find a tenant to lease the property from you, after three years when the property has appreciated to say, $200,000, you exercise your option to purchase. As the tenants have made thirty-six lease payments, they have contributed $21,600 ($600 x 36 months) toward your down payment, or 10.8 percent of the $200,000 purchase price. You obtain a loan of $128,400 ($150,000 - $21,600) for the remaining purchase price, creating instant equity of $71,600 ($200,000 - $128,400).

## *Technique 6*
### Buy low and refinance high

If you have excess cash sitting in a bank earning a mere three percent interest, or if you have just sold your principal residence and have pocketed a $500,000 gain on the sale or if you have access to OPM or have just obtained a home-equity line of credit (for investment purposes only), you may wish to utilize these funds to purchase properties at deep discounts of 80 to 75 percent of their fair market value. Once you have purchased the property, you can then go to a bank and obtain a new mortgage on the property, pull your money out of the property, and utilize the funds to purchase another property and repeat the process again and again.

For example, my wife and I found a seller, who for family reasons, needed to sell one of his rental properties quickly. The property was worth approximately $110,000, but he was willing to sell at a discount if we could close the transaction in one week. As a result, we were able to purchase the property for $80,000 by borrowing $80,000 from an associate who had money sitting in a bank earning 2.5 percent per year. We offered my associate a first mortgage on the home as security at an interest rate of 8 percent per year. The note was structured as an interest-only loan with a balloon payment in five years with no prepayment penalty. Within eighteen months we refinanced the home with a 4.75-percent, fifteen-year fixed mortgage and paid back our associate. Because our associate was so happy to earn a higher rate of interest, he has continued to lend money to us for further real estate investments.

While there are many more ways to purchase real estate creatively with little or no money down, it is not the purpose of this book to go into all of the various ways that you can purchase property. The point that I want to make is that even if at the present time you may not have a lot of capital to invest in real estate, don't let that stop you from pursuing your worry-free retirement. You can purchase real estate with little or no money down. While not all transactions lend themselves to this type of purchase structure, the deals do exist.

Lastly, there is no better time than a down market to be able to utilize these types of financing techniques. However, I caution you to be careful and to run your financial analysis of the proposed purchase with The Property Ledger in order to see if the transaction meets your investment criteria. Remember, you make money in real estate when you buy real estate, not when you sell it.

# Chapter 12

## Start Today On the Road
## Toward Your Worry-Free Retirement

As they say, "the journey of a thousand miles begins with the first step." The same is true in relation to the journey toward your worry-free retirement. It is my firm belief that the only way that you will be motivated enough to utilize the Real Estate Wealth-Building System to construct your Retirement Cash-Flow Solution is if you have awaken to the fact that no one will be there to build your retirement nest egg or to assist you with the majority of your retirement cash-flow needs—not the government, not social security, not Medicare, no one but yourself. This is the key decision that will motivate you to take action to start doing things differently to get a different result. The definition of insanity is doing the same thing over –and over and expecting a different result. You need to make the decision to make the Real Estate Wealth- Building System the cornerstone of your investment strategy in order to begin today to generate the types of appreciation, cash flow, and investment returns that will over time allow you to retire worry free.

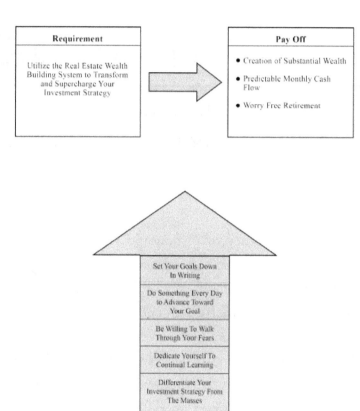

To that end, I suggest the following steps to get you started on the journey toward your worry-free retirement:

1. Complete the retirement vision worksheet form to determine the number of rental properties that will be required to provide for your Retirement Cash-Flow Solution.

2. Using the information provided in this book, register for the use of The Property Ledger to perform financial analyses, evaluate property acquisitions, and track your investment returns.

3. Set a goal in relation to the number of homes you wish to acquire on a yearly basis, and commit this goal to writing. Put the goal on your bathroom mirror so that you see the goal every morning and every evening.

4. Assess your financial resources to determine how much money you have to invest in rental properties.

5. Begin to assemble members of your Wealth Team, initially including a real estate agent, mortgage broker/banker, CPA, insurance broker, and possibly an attorney.

6. Meet with your mortgage broker/banker and check your credit score in order to determine what type of financing you may prequalify for in relation to the purchase of rental properties.

7. Begin to study your local real estate market utilizing the Real Estate Navigator forms that can be downloaded from The Property Ledger's website at www.thepropertyledger.com.

8. Review potential rental property acquisitions utilizing The Property Ledger to determine if the property's before and after tax cash-on-cash and internal rates of returns meet with your investment criteria.

9. Run multiple what-if scenarios to test the property's cash flow under different assumptions. Review The Property Ledger's Financial Dashboard to see how the rental property will add to your Retirement Cash-Flow Solution.

10. Acquire your first rental property and check the add to portfolio box on The Property Ledger to begin tracking the long-term financial performance of your rental properties;

11. Manage the property yourself. At this point, you will want to add a handyman to your Wealth Team;

12. Go to number 1 and repeat process. When you have acquired two or three rental properties, add a property manager to

your Wealth Team and turn over the property management function to the property manager.

13. Go back to number 1, and repeat the process until you have achieved your retirement vision.

Good luck and many happy returns as you take control of your financial destiny on your journey to financial freedom and a worry-free retirement!

# Free Offer—Two-Month Free Test Subscription to The Property Ledger

In order to access your free two-month test subscription to The Property Ledger, complete the following steps:

1. Go to www.thepropertyledger.com and click on the Resources tab.
2. Click on the Readers Only section.
3. Click on the Free Two-Month Subscription tab.
4. Within the Password box, type worryfreeretirement.
5. Hit return and follow the directions.

# Bibliography

Board of Governor's Federal Reserve. *Various Data Tables*, Federal Reserve, July 2008.

United States Bureau of Economic Analysis. *Various Data Tables*, United States Bureau of Economic Analysis, July 2008.

United States Bureau of Labor Statistics. *Various Data Tables*, United States Bureau of Labor Statistics, July 2008.

United States Census Bureau. *Various Data Tables*, United States Census Bureau, July 2008.

United States Bureau of Economic Analysis. *Various Data Tables*, United States Bureau of Economic Analysis, July 2008.

United States Office of Housing Enterprise Oversight. *Various Data Tables*, United States Office of Housing Enterprise Oversight July 2008.

www.inflation.com. *Various Data Tables*, www.inflation.com, July 2008.

www.moneycentral.com. *Various Data Tables*, www.moneycentral.com, July 2008.

www.trade-deficit.com. *Various Data Tables*, www.trade-deficit.com, July 2008.

# About the Author

**Carter Froelich** is the managing principal of the Phoenix office of a national real estate consulting firm. Carter is also the managing member of The Property Ledger, LLC, and creator of the web-based real estate software of the same name. Prior to assisting in the establishment of the national consulting firm in 1994, Carter was a consulting manager with the accounting and consulting firm of Kenneth Leventhal & Company in both the Newport Beach, California, and Phoenix, Arizona, offices.

Carter is a certified public accountant in the states of Arizona and California and is also an Arizona state certified general real estate appraiser. Carter received a master's degree in real estate development from the University of Southern California and holds a bachelor of science degree in business economics from the University of California at Santa Barbara.

Carter is a member of the Urban Land Institute, the Home Builders Association of Central Arizona, the Southern Arizona Home Builders Association, and the Building Contractor's Association of Idaho. Carter is a regular contributor to the Arizona School of Real Estate's monthly publication and has also served on the Camelback Village East Planning Board.

Carter lives with his wife, Bronwyn, and their three children in Phoenix, Arizona.

# BUY A SHARE OF THE FUTURE IN YOUR COMMUNITY

These certificates make great holiday, graduation and birthday gifts that can be personalized with the recipient's name. The cost of one S.H.A.R.E. or one square foot is $54.17. The personalized certificate is suitable for framing and will state the number of shares purchased and the amount of each share, as well as the recipient's name. The home that you participate in "building" will last for many years and will continue to grow in value.

**Here is a sample SHARE certificate:**

THIS CERTIFIES THAT

### YOUR NAME HERE

HAS INVESTED IN A HOME FOR A DESERVING FAMILY

**1985-2005**

TWENTY YEARS OF BUILDING FUTURES IN OUR
COMMUNITY ONE HOME AT A TIME

1200 SQUARE FOOT HOUSE @ $65,000 = $54.17 PER SQUARE FOOT
This certificate represents a tax deductible donation. It has no cash value.

## YES, I WOULD LIKE TO HELP!

*I support the work that Habitat for Humanity does and I want to be part of the excitement! As a donor, I will receive periodic updates on your construction activities but, more importantly, I know my gift will help a family in our community realize the dream of homeownership.* **I would like to SHARE in your efforts against substandard housing in my community!** *(Please print below)*

PLEASE SEND ME _____ SHARES at $54.17 EACH = $ $_____

*In Honor Of:* _____

*Occasion:* (Circle One)  HOLIDAY   BIRTHDAY   ANNIVERSARY

      OTHER: _____

*Address of Recipient:* _____

*Gift From:* _____ *Donor Address:* _____

*Donor Email:* _____

**I AM ENCLOSING A CHECK FOR $ $_____ PAYABLE TO HABITAT FOR HUMANITY OR PLEASE CHARGE MY VISA OR MASTERCARD** *(CIRCLE ONE)*

Card Number _____ Expiration Date: _____

Name as it appears on Credit Card _____ Charge Amount $ _____

Signature _____

Billing Address _____

Telephone # Day _____ Eve _____

**PLEASE NOTE:** Your contribution is tax-deductible to the fullest extent allowed by law.
**Habitat for Humanity • P.O. Box 1443 • Newport News, VA 23601 • 757-596-5553**
**www.HelpHabitatforHumanity.org**